SHAPES IN MATH, SCIENCE AND NATURE

CIRCLES

Written by Catherine Sheldrick Ross
Illustrated by Bill Slavin

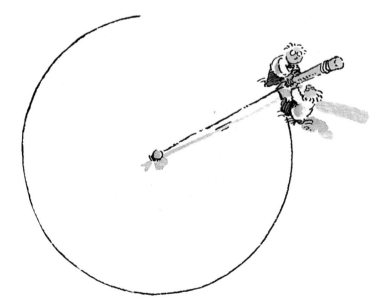

Kids Can Press Ltd.
Toronto

Kids Can Press Ltd. acknowledges with appreciation the assistance of the Canada Council and the Ontario Arts Council in the production of this book.

Canadian Cataloguing in Publication Data

Ross, Catherine Sheldrick
    Circles

Includes index.
ISBN 1-55074-064-4

1. Circle - Juvenile literature. I. Slavin, Bill.
II. Title.

QA484.R67 1992   j516'.15   C92-093260-6

Kids Can Press Ltd.
585 1/2 Bloor Street West
Toronto, Ontario, Canada
M6G 1K5

Edited by Laurie Wark
Designed by Michael Solomon
Typeset by Esperança Melo

92 0 9 8 7 6 5 4 3 2 1

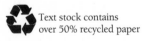 Text stock contains
over 50% recycled paper

Contents

Acknowledgements

Thanks are due to the many people who made this book possible. The mathematics specialists at Addison-Wesley and Houghton Mifflin provided excellent guidance on a proposal and early draft. Bruce Ross and Jacob Ross read various versions of the manuscript and made great suggestions. Professor Alistair Macdonald provided much-needed help with phyllotaxy. Susan Wallace rewrote some confusing directions. And D. B. Weldon interlibrary loan librarians worked hard to find elusive materials. Thanks also to the many children who helped to test out the activities. Of course, without the encouragement and patience of editors Laurie Wark and Valerie Wyatt and the design genius of Michael Solomon, there would be no book.

Introduction

What pattern do you see when you throw a stone into a still pond or look at the sawed-off stump of a tree? Circles. Look around — you likely see lots of circles. Circles are flat, with only two dimensions — length and width. But add a little thickness and you have a disc like a penny. Spin a penny around on its edge and you get a three-dimensional sphere with length, width and depth. The orange you eat for breakfast is a sphere, and so are the planets, soap bubbles, a drop of water — and maybe the universe itself. Take a circle, stretch it up into a column, and you have a cylinder. Tin cans are cylinders, and so are the trunks of trees and the bones in your legs.

You can make circles with your body—hugs are circles. Whirl around fast in one spot, and you are spinning in circles. Join hands with your friends, and you can do a circle dance.

When you read **Circles**, you will blow some super-bubbles; read about the most famous stone circle of all, Stonehenge; experiment to find out which shapes are strongest for constructing buildings; learn about things that spin, roll or twirl; find out why castles have round towers; discover what pine cones and sunflowers have in common; make some circle art; bake some yummy circles that you can eat; and much more.

If you find a circle word that you don't understand, check the glossary on page 78 for an explanation.

1 Amazing Circles

If you fold a circle in half anywhere, the two halves always exactly match. Try spinning a circle around like a wheel of fortune. It takes the same space as if it were standing still. If you roll a circle along the ground, it's always the same height. So circles make good wheels. Imagine riding a bicycle with square or triangular tires! Ouch! Circles are special because each point on a circle is exactly the same distance from the centre. This means that circles are perfectly symmetrical.

Giotto's O

Pope Benedict IX wanted to find the best painter in Italy to decorate the first St. Peter's Cathedral in Rome. So he sent a messenger to visit the great masters and get samples of their drawings. Finally the messenger arrived at Giotto's workshop in Florence where the painter was hard at work. When Giotto heard what the Pope wanted, he got out a fresh piece of paper and dipped his brush in red paint. Holding his arm close to his body, he made a perfect circle. "Here is your drawing," he said. The messenger thought Giotto was kidding and asked, "Won't you send anything else?" "Even this is too much," said Giotto. "Give it to the Pope along with all the other artists' drawings, and it will be appreciated." So the messenger gave the circle drawing to the Pope, explaining how it had been drawn freehand and without a compass. The

Pope and his art advisers recognized immediately Giotto's outstanding talent for drawing. And that's how Giotto came to Rome to paint for the Pope.

Drawing circles

Unless you are a Giotto, you might not be able to draw freehand a perfectly symmetrical circle, but here's how to drawn one with some simple equipment.

You'll need:
a compass
paper
a pencil
string
a pin

1. To draw a circle exactly the size you want, use a compass. Put the pointed end or foot of the compass on the paper just where you want the centre of the circle to be. Rotate the other end around it to draw your circle. Make sure the compass opening doesn't change in the middle of drawing your circle. (If it does change, the line you are drawing won't end up at its starting point and you won't have a circle.)

2. To make bigger or smaller circles, change the distance between the two compass feet. The circle you draw will always be twice as wide as the distance between the two compass feet — this distance is the circle's radius.

3. To draw bigger circles than your compass will allow, you can use a pencil and string. Tie one end of the string around the pencil. Use a pin to hold the other end of the string to the centre of your paper. Pull the string tight and draw a line around the pin until you get back to your starting point. To draw a really big circle on pavement, you can use this same string method. Tie one end of the string around a piece of chalk. Get a friend to hold the other end on the ground. Pull the string tight and draw the line.

THE CIRCLE UP CLOSE

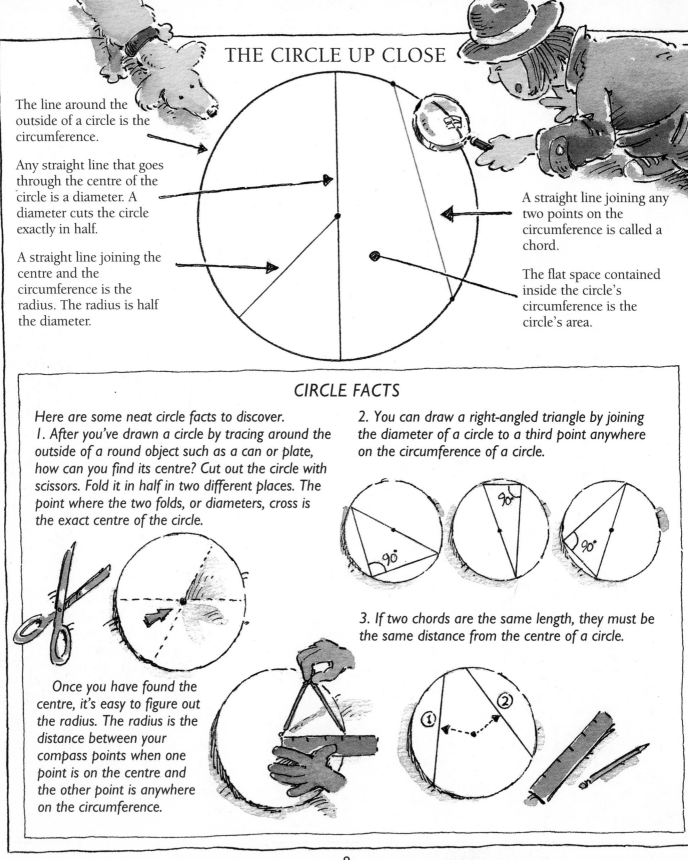

The line around the outside of a circle is the circumference.

Any straight line that goes through the centre of the circle is a diameter. A diameter cuts the circle exactly in half.

A straight line joining the centre and the circumference is the radius. The radius is half the diameter.

A straight line joining any two points on the circumference is called a chord.

The flat space contained inside the circle's circumference is the circle's area.

CIRCLE FACTS

Here are some neat circle facts to discover.
1. After you've drawn a circle by tracing around the outside of a round object such as a can or plate, how can you find its centre? Cut out the circle with scissors. Fold it in half in two different places. The point where the two folds, or diameters, cross is the exact centre of the circle.

Once you have found the centre, it's easy to figure out the radius. The radius is the distance between your compass points when one point is on the centre and the other point is anywhere on the circumference.

2. You can draw a right-angled triangle by joining the diameter of a circle to a third point anywhere on the circumference of a circle.

3. If two chords are the same length, they must be the same distance from the centre of a circle.

Fold some circles

What can you do with circles you have drawn? Try folding them to make some other great shapes — triangles, squares, hexagons, even stars.

1. Use a compass to draw a circle on your paper. Don't make your circle too small — set your compass points about 10 cm (4 inches) apart. This distance will be the radius of your circle. Cut out the circle.

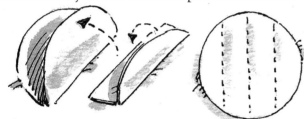

2. Fold the circle in half. Fold it in half again parallel to, or alongside, the first fold. Open the circle out and you will see three parallel fold lines.

3. Now fold the circle in half again so that your new fold line intersects, or cuts across, the other folds at right angles as shown. Fold it in half again as before.

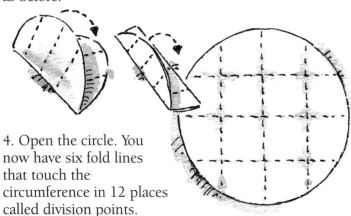

4. Open the circle. You now have six fold lines that touch the circumference in 12 places called division points.

5. Use your ruler to draw lines to connect these 12 division points. Connect every point and you get a 12-sided polygon. Mathematicians call this 12-sided shape a **dodecagon**.

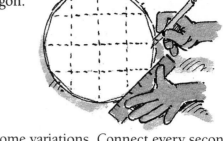

6. Try some variations. Connect every second point to get a hexagon (six sides). Connect every third point (skip two) and you get a square. Connect every fourth point (skip three) to get a triangle.

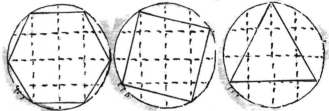

7. If you want to get fancy, make this star pattern. Pick a division point and look for a second point exactly opposite it along the diameter. Connect your first point with the two division points on either side of the second point. For example, connect point 12 with points 5 and 7. Repeat for each division point.

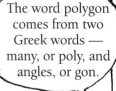

The word polygon comes from two Greek words — many, or poly, and angles, or gon.

Measuring circles

Suppose you had something circular like a plate and you wanted to know how big it was. How could you measure it? If you knew the circle's radius (see page 8 for one way of finding out the radius), it would be easy to double the radius to get the diameter. This way you'd know how big the circle is across the middle. But you might also want to know how big the circle is around the outside — its circumference. Or how much space there is inside the circle — its area.

Look at these two plates. It's easy to see that the plate with the bigger diameter also has a bigger circumference with more area inside it. But how much more? And how can you measure it? With an amazing number called pi (named for the Greek letter π and pronounced pie). Thousands of years ago, mathematicians made the discovery that no matter how big a circle is, the number you get by dividing its circumference by its diameter is always the same. This number is called pi.

Here's how you can figure out the approximate value of pi.

You'll need:
a piece of string
a cylinder (such as a can)
scissors
a pencil
paper

1. Wrap a piece of string tightly around the cylinder. Cut the string so that it is exactly long enough to go around the cylinder. (This string will be the length of the circumference of the cylinder.)

2. Trace the outline of the bottom of the cylinder on a piece of paper and cut out the circle.

3. Fold the circle in half to make a diameter.

4. Hold the string taut, match the diameter against the string, and note the end point. Starting at this end point, match the diameter against the string again as before. Repeat until you run out of string. How many diameters could you fit along the length of string?

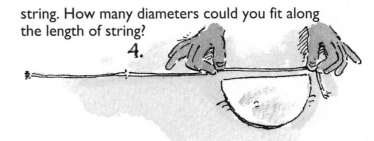

What's happening?
You probably made the diameter fit three times along the string and then had a bit of string left over. So the circumference divided by the diameter, or pi, is a bit more than three. The ancient Greeks worked out the value of pi to four decimal places — 3.1416.

As long as you know the value of pi, there's only one more thing you really need to know to measure a circle — its radius. Knowing pi and the circle's radius, you can always figure out its circumference and its area.

The circumference is two times pi (π) multiplied by the radius (r). That's $2 \times \pi \times r$ or $2\pi r$.

The area of a circle (the amount of space contained inside the circle) is pi times the radius multiplied by itself. That's $\pi \times r \times r$ or πr^2.

SPACE TEST

Put a penny on the table. How many other pennies can you fit around the first penny, touching it? Do you get the same answer if you try this space test using dimes? How about quarters?

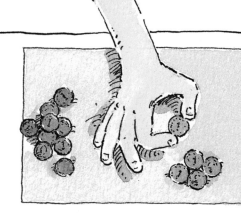

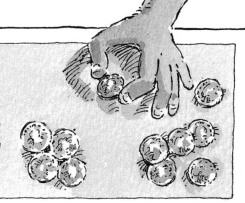

Easy as pi

Gravestone π

Working out pi more accurately than 3.1416 is time-consuming and not very useful. (Ten decimals are enough to calculate the circumference of a sphere the size of the Earth.) But some mathematicians can't turn down a challenge. Leudolph van Ceulen, a Dutch mathematician, spent much of his life calculating pi to 35 decimal places. When he died in 1610, the numbers 2 8 8 were carved on his tombstone — the thirty-third, thirty-fourth and thirty-fifth decimal places of π.

A π record

π = 3.14159265358979323846264338327950288 41971693993751058209749445923078164062 86208998628034825 and so on forever. So what is now the most accurate measurement of pi? Two brothers, David and Gregory Chudnovsky, passed the 1-billion mark in 1989. To print out the value of π to this many decimal points would take a stack of computer paper 20 times as high as a tall man. The world record for calculating the value of π never lasts very long because there is no final answer — the decimal places go on forever.

Sci fi π

On an episode of "Star Trek," Spock used π to outwit a smart but nasty computer. This out-of-control computer had decided to destroy the Starship Enterprise. Spock tricked the computer by asking it to figure out the value for pi. Since this calculation goes on forever, it kept the evil computer very busy. Meanwhile, the crew had time to discover how to shut the computer down.

π memory test

How many numbers in the value of pi can you remember? Most people can get to 3.14 or possibly to 3.1416. Since the value for pi is a string of numbers that goes on forever with no pattern, it's impossible to memorize. But in 1987 a Japanese man recited from memory the value for pi to 40 000 places. According to The *Guinness Book of Records*, it took him 17 hours and 21 minutes, including 4 1/4 hours of breaks.

CIRCLE IMPOSSIBILITIES

Then in 1989 Miklos Laczkovich of Hungary apparently discovered a new way of squaring the circle — by cutting up the circle into tiny pieces and rearranging them into a square. He figured that to make a square with no gaps and no overlapping pieces would take 10^{50} pieces. That's 10 multiplied by itself 50 times.

Mathematicians like challenges and don't give up easily. Calculating the final value of π isn't their only impossible circle challenge. There's also "squaring the circle." People have been trying for 4000 years to make a square that encloses an area exactly equal to the area of a given circle, using only a ruler and compass. By 1775 so many crackpots were trying to square the circle that the French Academy declared it wouldn't examine any more solutions to this puzzle. No one has ever succeeded in squaring the circle with a ruler and compass, and no one ever will. In 1882 a German mathematician proved the task was impossible.

Why do elephants have round feet?

To step on the lily pads.

Why is an aspirin small, white and circular?

Because if it were big, grey and wrinkly, it would be an elephant.

Make a Moebius strip

Here's a neat circle trick that turns an ordinary strip of paper into an incredible loop.

You'll need:
a strip of paper about 30 cm (12 inches) long and 2 cm (1 inch) wide
tape
a coloured marker
scissors

1. Take a strip of paper and bring the ends together. Give one end a half-turn and tape the ends together. You've made a Moebius strip.

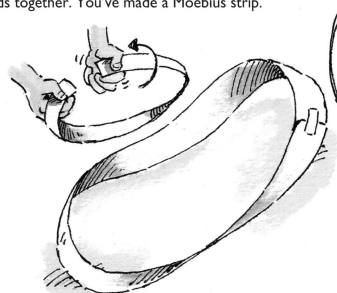

2. Draw a line along the paper band down its middle. Start anywhere and keep going, without lifting your marker, until you get back to your starting place. Surprised? Which side is "inside" and which is "outside"? Your line goes along both sides and yet you did not cross an edge. This means your loop has only one side. An ant would be able to walk on it from any spot to any other spot without ever crossing an edge.

3. Try something else. Cut along the line you drew. If you cut an ordinary loop of paper through the middle, it separates into two narrower loops. How many sides does the cut-in-half Moebius strip have? (To find out, draw a line as before along the length of the band till you get back to your starting place.) How many twists does it have now?

What's happening?

The Moebius strip has only one surface and one edge. The German mathematician, August Ferdinand Moebius, wrote about it in 1858 as an amusing game, but the Moebius strip has turned out to have practical uses. Engineers use them as conveyor belts on assembly lines. An ordinary belt, with an inside and an outside, wears out faster on one side than the other. A Moebius strip, with only one side, wears evenly and lasts longer.

2 Living in Circles

Imagine what it would be like to be completely circle shaped. Instead of having a head and arms and feet and walking upright, you would just roll over and over. That's what the first life forms did. Small ball-shaped creatures, like this radiolarian, lived in the sea, rolling and tossing in the current, with no upside-down and no right way up. Just like circles, they had what's called radial symmetry — they looked exactly the same from every direction.

Then life branched off along two different paths. Some life forms became plants, which also have radial symmetry, and some became animals. Take a look at your own body — does it have radial symmetry? Of course not. You definitely have a right-side-up, and your left eye is matched by a right eye; your left arm and leg are matched by a right arm and leg. Your left side is the mirror image of your right side, so your body has bilateral symmetry.

Check out these two different kinds of symmetry for yourself. Fold a piece of paper in half and cut out a half circle and doll as shown. When you unfold these shapes, you should have a full circle and paper doll.

Now fold the circle in half along different fold lines. You can fold it in half anywhere, and the two halves will always match up. That's radial symmetry — symmetry in all directions. Now fold the doll in half down the centre. The two halves will match — that centre fold line is called the axis of symmetry.

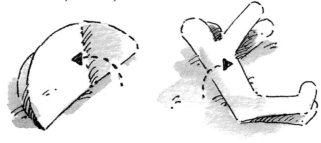

What happens if you fold the doll in half any other way? It won't match up. Like your body, the doll has bilateral symmetry with only one axis of symmetry. When you folded your circle, you discovered that it has more than one axis of symmetry.

So why do plants have radial symmetry, while animals have bilateral symmetry? It's because plants stay in one place, and animals move around. Since plants stay rooted, they don't need a front and a back, a right side and a left side. Instead, nearly identical parts grow out from the centre in all directions, like the branches on a pine tree. So trees and bushes usually are circular. But since animals move, most have evolved into shapes with bilateral symmetry. A moving animal needs special features on the front of its body. You may have heard jokes about teachers with eyes in the back of their heads. But of course eyes, ears and nose all point frontward — an animal needs to know where it is going towards, not where it is coming from. Since enemies are just as likely to spring from the left as from the right, an animal needs all the same features on its left side as on its right. So, in your own body, your front is very different from your back, but your left side and your right side are mirror images of each other.

Circle prints

Plants grow in circles, and you can find circle shapes in parts of plants too, such as in fruits and vegetables. Jazz up your notepaper and wrapping paper with these circle designs.

You'll need:
a knife
fruit or vegetables such as oranges, lemons, apples, onions, cucumbers, carrots, radishes
paint brushes
tempera paint (various colours)
paper (If you want to make wrapping paper, use large pieces of recycled newsprint.)

1. To make your circle-shaped stamps, cut an apple or an orange in half. Cut thick cross-sections, or slices, from onions, carrots or cucumbers (if you make them too thin, they're hard to hold when you use them as stamps). You might also want to cut a few carrot slices in half to make semi-circles.

2. Use a brush to apply paint to a circle stamp, or dip the stamp into the paint.

3. Press the stamp onto the paper. Don't move it sideways or the paint will blur.

4. Keep making impressions with the same stamp until you run out of paint. With onion or orange stamps, the texture shows through when the paint runs out, making an interesting design.

5. When the paint on the stamp has been used up, apply more. Experiment with different shapes and designs, different colours and different amounts of paint on the stamp.

CIRCLE SIGNS

We don't know exactly what cave dwellers meant when they scratched circle signs onto their cave walls. But we do know that from very early times, the circle has been a powerful sign. Here are some of the things that circles have meant.

TO MYTH MAKERS

God, eternity, fire

Water

Sun, Earth

TO ROMANS WRITING NUMBERS

Roman numeral for 500

Roman numeral for 1000. Eventually this number was written as M, which is the way it now appears in dates at the end of Hollywood movies.

TO METEOROLOGISTS PREDICTING THE WEATHER

Clear sky

Cloudy sky

TO BOTANISTS TALKING ABOUT FLOWERS

Annual plants living for only one year

Male flower

Female flower

TO ENVIRONMENTALISTS CARING FOR THE EARTH

This recycling sign suggests using something over and over. Look for it on books, paper and boxes that you buy. It means the paper is made from other paper that has been used before.

Building in circles

Take a piece of string and tie the ends together to form a loop. Put the loop on a table and push it around into different positions — a square, a rectangle, a triangle, a circle. What shape should you make the loop if you want to enclose the largest area possible inside the loop?

Princess Dido knew the answer to this puzzle. According to an ancient Greek legend, her brother Pygmalion murdered her husband. Dido fled with some loyal supporters to the coast of north Africa near modern Tunis. She asked the local king to sell her some land so that she could build a new city there. When he said no, she won him over by saying, "Just sell me the amount of land that I can enclose by the hide of an ox." As soon as the king agreed, Dido told her servants to tan an ox-hide and cut it up into long, very narrow strips. Then she sewed all the strips together to make one very

long leather strip. With this strip, she formed a loop large enough to enclose land for building the new city of Carthage. What shape was Dido's loop? A circle. A loop will contain the most area inside if the loop is in the shape of a circle.

The super circle

Use Queen Dido's cutting trick to amaze your friends. Show them that, with nothing but scissors, you can cut an ordinary index card into a circle big enough to step through.

You'll need:
an 8 x 13 cm (3 x 5 inch) index card
scissors

1. Fold the card in half so that the short edges meet.

2. Cut through the folded card as shown. Your first cut should start at the fold. Leave .5 cm (1/4 inch) uncut.

3. Make your second cut alongside the first cut, but this time start your cut on the opposite side of the card. As before, leave .5 cm (1/4 inch) uncut.

4. Alternate your cuts from side to side until you have made cuts in the whole card as shown. You should end up with an odd number of cuts (13 or 15 cuts but not 12 or 14). The closer together you make the cuts, the more cuts you'll have and the bigger your super circle will be.

5. Unfold the card and flatten it out. You now have an interesting chain, but to do the magic circle trick you need to make one more cut. Cut through all the folds except for the ones at each end of the card. Voilà! A large loop you can squeeze your whole body through. (If you want to get a cow through your magic circle with lots of room to spare, start with a sheet of exercise paper and make your cuts quite close together.)

Round towns

When a herd of Arctic musk-oxen want to fend off wolves and bears, how do they stand? In a circle. The adults face outward, ready to use their horns and sharp hooves against enemies. Baby and young musk-oxen are kept safe inside the circle. People also, from the earliest times, have used circles for building protected spaces to live in. In Egyptian hieroglyphics, the oldest writing system that can still be read, the symbol for city is a circle with a cross inside.

One reason for designing round towns is that the circle is considered a perfect shape, representing wholeness and harmony. But another reason is that circular towns are easiest to defend, and it takes the least possible amount of bricks and stones for the outside walls. If you compare towns of the same size, the wall around the circular town will always be shorter than the wall around a town of any other shape. Here are some famous circular towns.

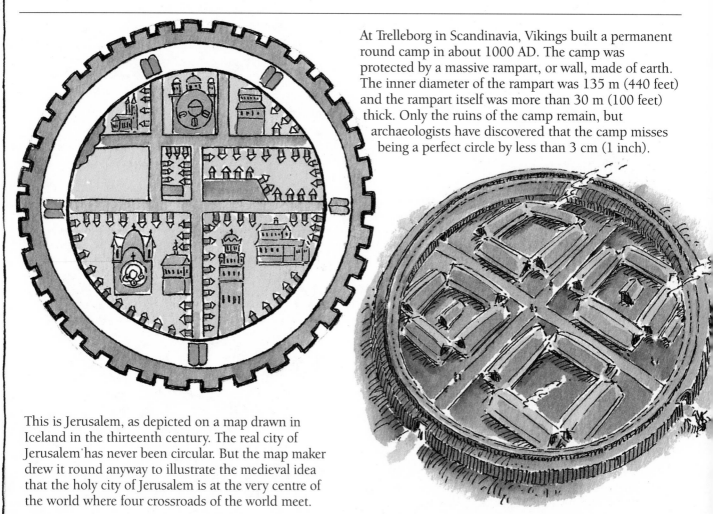

At Trelleborg in Scandinavia, Vikings built a permanent round camp in about 1000 AD. The camp was protected by a massive rampart, or wall, made of earth. The inner diameter of the rampart was 135 m (440 feet) and the rampart itself was more than 30 m (100 feet) thick. Only the ruins of the camp remain, but archaeologists have discovered that the camp misses being a perfect circle by less than 3 cm (1 inch).

This is Jerusalem, as depicted on a map drawn in Iceland in the thirteenth century. The real city of Jerusalem has never been circular. But the map maker drew it round anyway to illustrate the medieval idea that the holy city of Jerusalem is at the very centre of the world where four crossroads of the world meet.

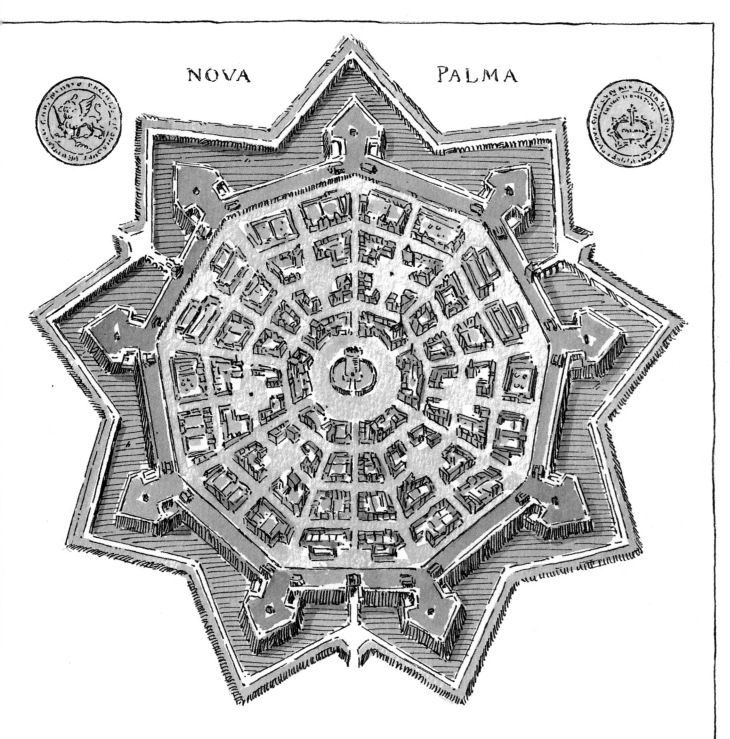

NOVA　　PALMA

In the fifteenth and sixteenth centuries in Europe, a lot more circular cities were planned than were actually built. Town planners wrote many books saying that the round city was the ideal form, harmonious and perfect. They said it was the form used by Nature herself when she made honeycomb cells and birds' nests. The Italian fortress city of Palmanova was actually built starting in 1593 and has kept its circular shape right up to the present.

When the Canada Land Company wanted to settle part of its tract of bush on Lake Huron in 1826, it used this round plan for Goderich, Ontario. You can see that all of the streets radiate from a central circular area. To the settlers who made their home there, this city plan must have seemed like an island of safety and order in the middle of the dangerous wilderness.

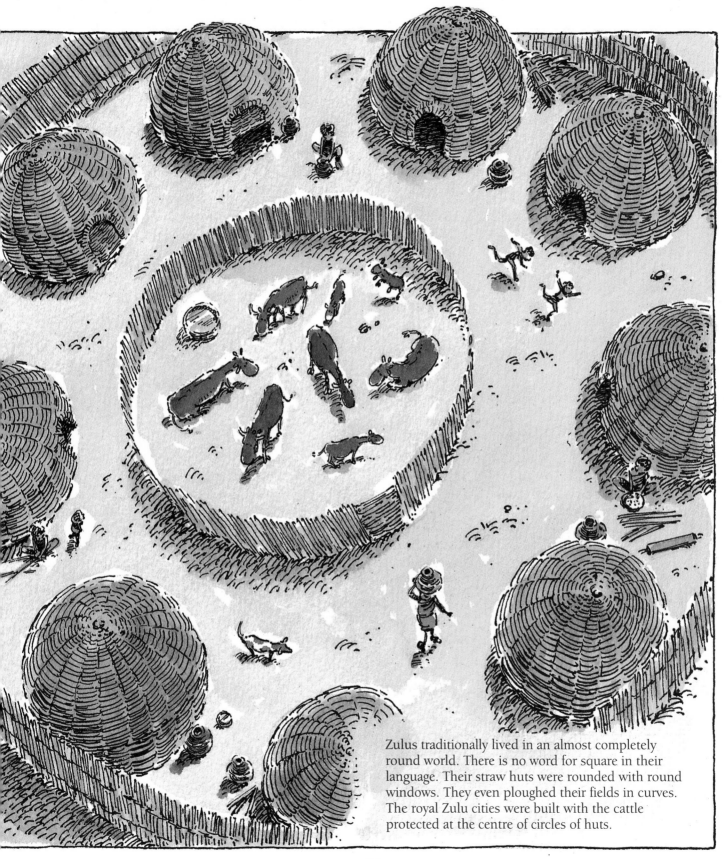

Zulus traditionally lived in an almost completely round world. There is no word for square in their language. Their straw huts were rounded with round windows. They even ploughed their fields in curves. The royal Zulu cities were built with the cattle protected at the centre of circles of huts.

Circle art

Since the first cave dwellers began drawing circle signs, the circle has been a favourite with artists and designers. Make some dazzling patterns with these circle designs that are thousands of years old.

Yin and Yang

Think of some opposites — light and dark, dry and wet, male and female. For the Chinese, all these matched pairs are summed up in the Yin and Yang. This 3000-year-old Chinese design represents the marriage of forces in the universe that are opposite, but equally strong.

You'll need:
a pencil
a compass
white paper
a ruler
a black coloured marker

1. Draw a circle on white paper with a radius of about 5 cm (2 inches). Label the centre of the circle C.

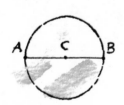

2. Draw a diameter by drawing a line through C to intersect the circumference at A and B.

3. Don't change the compass opening. Put the compass foot on point A and draw two arcs or curved lines to intersect the circumference, one above and and one below the diameter line as shown.

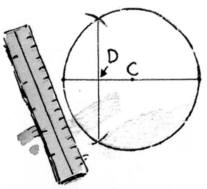

4. With a ruler, draw a line to connect the intersection points. This line bisects (cuts in half) the radius at a point we can label D.

5. Use the distance between A and D as the radius of a smaller

semi-circle that has its centre at D. Draw the semi-circle above the diameter line.

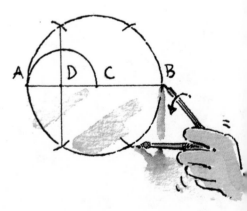

6. Using the radius of the original large circle, put the compass foot on point B and draw two arcs to intersect the circumference, one above and one below the diameter line.

— 24 —

7. Draw a line to connect the intersection points as before to bisect the radius at a point we can label E.

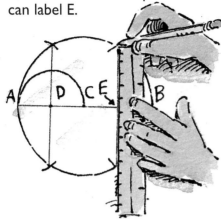

8. Use the distance between A and E as the radius of a smaller semi-circle that has its centre

at E. Draw the semi-circle below the diameter line.

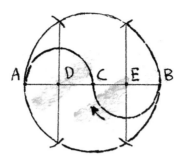

9. Colour the top part of the circle black as shown to be the Yin and leave the other half white to be the Yang.

10. Don't forget the dots. The ancient Chinese thought that

the opposite forces of the universe could never be completely separate. And so the Yang has a bit of Yin in it, and the Yin, of course, contains a bit of Yang. Colour a black dot on the white Yang and leave a white dot uncoloured on the black Yin.

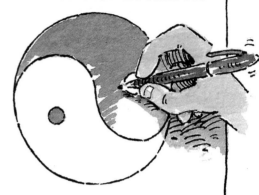

Catherine Wheel

Have you ever watched a pinwheel firework that spins around and gives off sparks? Then you've seen a Catherine Wheel, named after the fourth-century Christian, Saint Catherine. According to legend, she was condemned to die on a burning wheel but was saved at the last minute by a miracle. Celebrate Saint Catherine with this pinwheel design.

You'll need:
a pencil
a compass
white paper
a ruler

1. Follow the steps to draw the Yin and Yang.

2. Draw a second diameter as shown, perpendicular to the first one.

3. Repeat all the steps for drawing the Yin and Yang on the second diameter.

Petals

Flowers with six petals don't occur very often in nature. But you can make them easily by drawing these interlocking circles with your compass.

You'll need:
a compass
a pencil
white paper
a ruler
some coloured markers or
    pencil crayons

1. Use your compass to draw a circle on white paper.

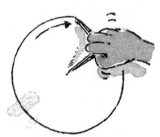

2. Keep the same compass opening that you used for the radius of your circle. Mark a point on the circumference. Put the compass foot on this point and draw an arc to intersect the circle. This point of intersection is called a division point.

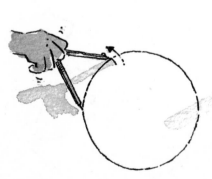

3. Continue working your way around the circumference of the circle, using the radius to mark four more division points. You now have divided the circle into six equal parts at these six division points.

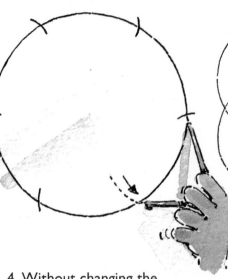

4. Without changing the compass opening, draw a second circle by putting the compass foot on one of the division points. This new circle goes through the centre of the old circle as well as through two division points.

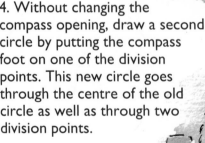

5. Draw five more circles with centres on the other division points. If you have been careful not to change the compass opening, you will have seven perfect interlocking circles.

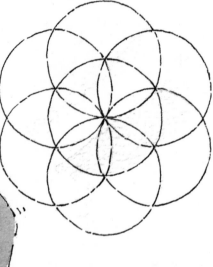

6. Colour your pattern to make it look like stained glass.

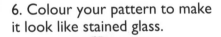

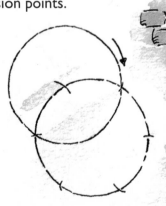

Tiling

A circle is the starting point for special shapes that you can use to make great designs. Using these shapes, your designs will fit together perfectly, without any overlapping and without leaving gaps. Mathematicians call it tiling, and they know that only certain shapes will work to cover a surface without leaving spaces in between. Our pioneer grandmothers knew these shapes, too, and used them for the pieces in their quilts. Here's how to make some of them.

You'll need:
a compass
a pencil
Bristol board or cardboard in
    different colours
a ruler
scissors

1. Use your compass to draw a circle on a piece of cardboard. A radius of 5 cm (2 inches) works well.

2. Use your compass to mark six division points, as in Steps 2 and 3 of Petals (see page 26).

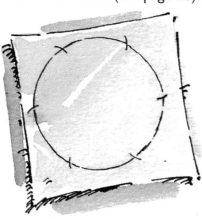

3. With your ruler, draw lines to join the division points. Now you have a hexagon — a six-sided shape.

4. Use this cardboard hexagon as a pattern to cut out two more identical cardboard hexagons.

5. Cut up one hexagon as shown to make a triangle and a diamond pattern. Construct a square on one of the sides of the second hexagon. Cut out the square.

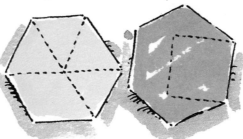

6. Now use these cardboard patterns to cut hexagons, squares, diamonds and triangles from Bristol board. Use a different colour for each shape. If you cut out at least 10 of each shape, you'll have enough to make some intricate designs. You might want to try these, which come from a book by Johannes Kepler published in 1619.

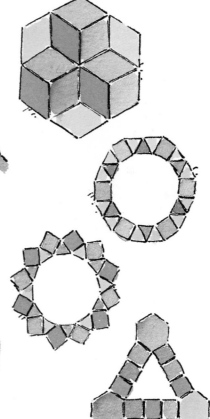

3 Far-out circles

You may not feel that you're moving, but you're actually whirling around the sun at an average rate of almost 30 km (19 miles) a second. Our sun is also hurtling through our star system, the Milky Way, at about 19 km (12 miles) per second, along with 100 billion other suns that we call stars. The Milky Way goes in circles, too, making one turn every 200 million years. So the universe is one grand circle dance of whirling, twirling, circling and spinning.

It took many centuries of star-gazing to figure out this circle dance. The ancient Greek astronomer Ptolemy in the second century AD thought that the Earth was right at the centre of everything in the universe. It's natural to want to be in the most important place. If you had your choice, where would you rather be? Off somewhere on the edge or right at the centre of things? Ptolemy knew where he preferred to be. He claimed that the Earth stood still and that everything else circled around it. People believed him for more than 1500 years.

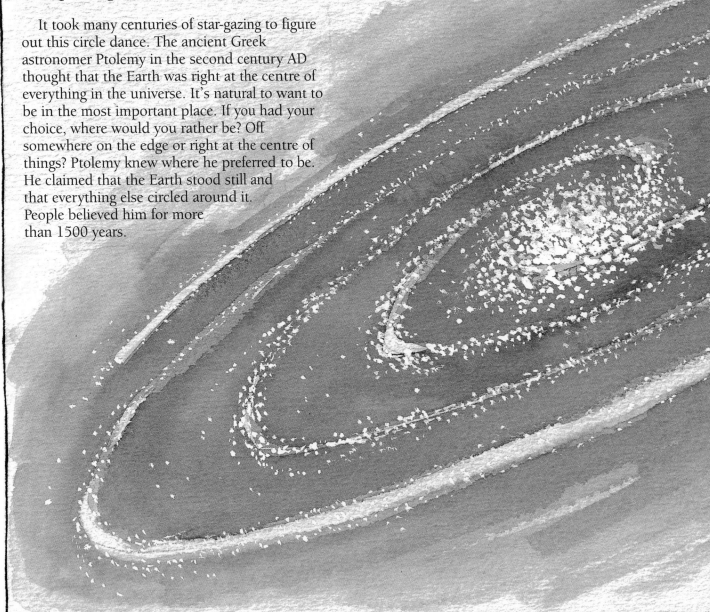

In Ptolemy's system, the Earth was the centre of the universe. The planets moved in circles around the Earth.

Copernicus put the sun at the centre.

Kepler found that each planet travels in an elliptical orbit around the sun.

Then, almost 500 years ago, the Polish astronomer Copernicus shocked everybody with his revolutionary idea that the sun sits at the centre, while the Earth circles around the sun. He said that the sun only seems to be moving across the sky each day. Really the Earth does the moving. His picture of the universe shows an unmoving sun at the centre of seven circles that are the orbits of the planets. Why circular orbits? Because the circle represents perfection. According to Copernicus, the Creator would surely choose the most perfect form there is. When people heard Copernicus's new theory, they thought he was crazy. How could the Earth be hurtling around the sun at high speed? Why doesn't the moon get left behind and lost? Why don't we feel any motion?

And why don't all the trees and houses and people fall off the Earth?

Shortly after 1600, the German astronomer Johannes Kepler made another startling breakthrough. All the planets move around the sun, just as Copernicus had said, but they don't move in a circle. The planets actually move in an ellipse. An ellipse is like a flattened circle with two centres instead of one. Kepler also discovered that the sun was at one centre or focus of the elliptical orbits of the planets. Kepler used the word focus for the ellipse because focus means fireplace or hearth in Latin. The sun, like a fireplace, is the source of light and heat for all the planets in our solar system.

Make an ellipse

An ellipse looks like a circle that's been sat on. It's easy to make. If you draw a circle on a stretchy rubbery substance, you can turn it into an ellipse by stretching out the circle in one direction. But a better way is to use the string method.

You'll need:
a piece of string about 25 cm (10 inches) long
a sheet of paper
a corkboard
2 thumbtacks
a pencil

1. Tie the string together at the ends to form a loop.

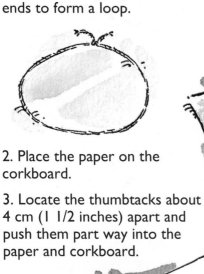

2. Place the paper on the corkboard.

3. Locate the thumbtacks about 4 cm (1 1/2 inches) apart and push them part way into the paper and corkboard.

4. Loop the string around the thumbtacks. Put a pencil inside the string loop and pull tight.

5. Keeping the string pulled tight, draw a curve with your pencil until you come back to your starting point. An ellipse!

6. Experiment. You can make bigger or smaller ellipses by changing the length of the string you use to make the loop. You can also get different results by moving the thumbtacks further apart or closer together. The thumbtacks are the foci or centres of your ellipse. What happens if you put your thumbtacks really close together?

The expanding circle trick

Challenge your friends to the expanding circle mystery.

You'll need:
a pencil
a dime
an index card
scissors
a quarter

1. Trace the outline of a dime on the index card.

2. Carefully cut out around the outline, making a dime-sized hole in the card.

3. Ask your friends to push the quarter through the hole without ripping the card. Impossible? Show them how.

4. Fold the card along the diameter of the cut-out circle. Put the quarter between the folds in the card so that it sticks out the hole in the card. The hole is too small to let the quarter go through.

5. Bend the fold of the card down as shown. Now the quarter passes through easily.

How does it work?
By bending the card, you turn the circle into an ellipse with a bigger diameter — big enough to let the quarter slip through.

Stone circles

About 900 stone circles are still left in England from prehistoric times, but Stonehenge is the biggest and most famous of these mysterious constructions. This circle of huge stones is so mind-boggling that 1 million people visit it every year. How did it get there and why was it built? Some people used to say that Stonehenge was made by Egyptian pyramid builders who came to England. Others said it was made by Martians. But many astronomers now think that Stonehenge was built by prehistoric people as a huge observatory to watch the sun, identify the longest day of the year and even predict eclipses of the moon.

We now know that Stonehenge was actually made in stages over a very long period. Stone-age people began the outer part almost 4500 years ago. At first they dug a circular ditch. Inside the ditch, they built a circular wall with an inside diameter of about 97 m (320 feet) — almost the length of a football field. This wall of earth was

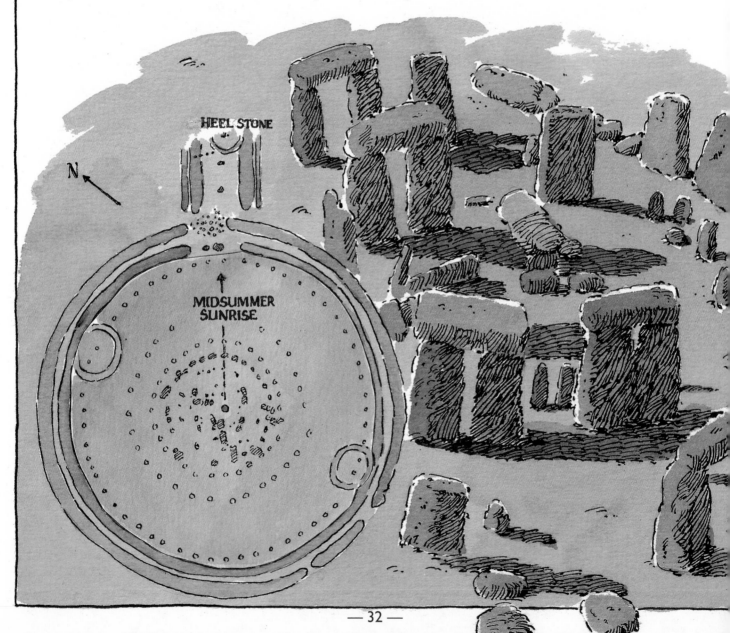

about 6 m (20 feet) thick and as high as a tall person — that's a lot of earth to move with only deer antler picks and other primitive equipment. Workers left a gap in the wall so that people at the centre of the circle could look out and see a huge rock, called the Heelstone, outside the circle. The line that joins the centre of the circle to the Heelstone points to the rising sun on June 21 — the longest day of the year, when the days begin to get shorter.

The famous inner circle of huge stones wasn't built for another 1000 years, by different people with a different language. Its huge upright stones, each weighing as much as 12 Indian elephants, had to be dragged 30 km (19 miles) over hilly country to the Stonehenge site. Cross pieces, or lintels, were fitted on top of the upright stones. Amazingly, five of these lintels are still in place, even after 3500 years. At dawn on the summer solstice on June 21, you can look from the centre of the circle through the stone archway to the Heelstone and see the rising sun.

MYSTERY CIRCLES

Scientists are baffled by mystery circles that have been appearing in farmers' fields. Something has been flattening out crops of wheat and barley to form perfect circles. In 1990 more than 400 circles were counted in southern England alone, some as big as 60 m (197 feet) in diameter. Crop circles are not new. They were spotted during the Middle Ages by people who thought they were the work of "mowing devils." Now some people say the circles are doodles drawn by extraterrestrials, while others think the crops are being flattened into circles by hundreds of mating hedgehogs. However, most scientists insist there has to be a better explanation — they just don't agree on what the explanation is. So far, the most likely theory seems to be that whirling winds touch down in fields and leave behind the mysterious circles. Meanwhile, Britain's Centre for Crop Circle Studies is still collecting evidence.

Make a sundial

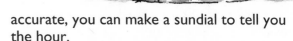

You don't have to build a Stonehenge to track the sun. You can put a stick in the ground in full sunshine and watch how the shadow moves. In the early morning, the shadow is long and points west, away from the sun. At noon, when the sun is overhead, the shadow is short. Towards evening, the shadow lengthens again and points east. So a stick in the ground can give you a rough idea of the time of day. For something more accurate, you can make a sundial to tell you the hour.

You need two essential parts for a sundial: the shadow maker and the dial. The shadow maker is called the gnomon (a Greek word meaning one who knows). The shadow falls on a surface with markings on it, called the dial (from the Latin word *dies*, meaning day).

You'll need:
a ruler
a pencil
a square piece of corrugated
  cardboard 30 cm × 30 cm
  (12 inches × 12 inches)
a compass
a protractor
an oblong piece of corrugated
  cardboard at least 12 cm ×
  30 cm (5 inches × 12 inches)
scissors
masking tape

1. Use your ruler to draw a line connecting the midpoints of two sides of the cardboard square. Use the sharp point of the compass to score along this line (don't press hard enough to tear the cardboard). Fold along the scored line.

2. Draw a line parallel to a third side 2 cm (1 inch) in from the edge. Measure to find the midpoint of this line.

3. Put the compass foot on the midpoint and, below the line, draw a semi-circle with a radius of 10 cm (4 inches).

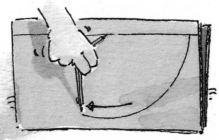

4. To turn this semi-circle into a dial, you need to divide the semi-circle into 12 equal units. Line up your protractor on the semi-circle as shown, with the centre of the protractor on the centre of the semi-circle. Read the markings on the outside curve of the protractor, and put a mark on your dial every 15° — where it says 15, 30, 45, 60, 75, 90, etc. — until you have marked off 11 equally spaced points on the outside of the semi-circle.

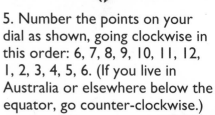

5. Number the points on your dial as shown, going clockwise in this order: 6, 7, 8, 9, 10, 11, 12, 1, 2, 3, 4, 5, 6. (If you live in Australia or elsewhere below the equator, go counter-clockwise.)

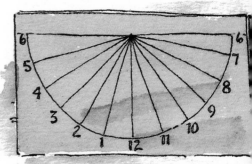

6. Use the sharp foot of the compass to poke a hole through the cardboard at the centre of the semi-circle. Push a pencil through the hole. This pencil is your gnomon or shadow maker. When you get your sundial finished, the gnomon will end up being held at an angle equal to the latitude where you live.

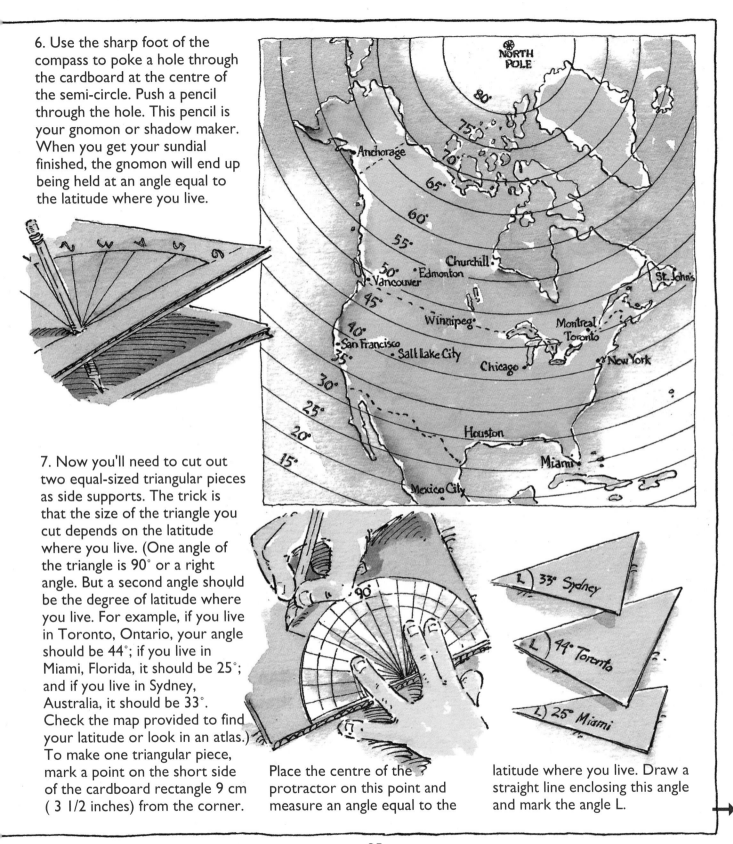

7. Now you'll need to cut out two equal-sized triangular pieces as side supports. The trick is that the size of the triangle you cut depends on the latitude where you live. (One angle of the triangle is 90° or a right angle. But a second angle should be the degree of latitude where you live. For example, if you live in Toronto, Ontario, your angle should be 44°; if you live in Miami, Florida, it should be 25°; and if you live in Sydney, Australia, it should be 33°. Check the map provided to find your latitude or look in an atlas.) To make one triangular piece, mark a point on the short side of the cardboard rectangle 9 cm (3 1/2 inches) from the corner.

Place the centre of the protractor on this point and measure an angle equal to the latitude where you live. Draw a straight line enclosing this angle and mark the angle L.

8. Cut out the triangle. Trace this triangle on the leftover piece of cardboard and cut out a second triangle the same as the first. Mark the angle L.

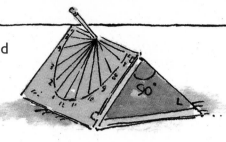

10. Fit the second triangle in and secure it with masking tape. Make sure that the angle marked L is on the side of the base away from the fold in the cardboard dial.

11. Now you are ready to try out your sundial. Pick a spot for your sundial where the sun shines all day. Align the sundial with the tip of the gnomon, or pencil, facing north (south if you live south of the equator). An easy way to line up your sundial correctly the first time is to use your watch — turn the sundial so that the shadow indicates the right time. But if it's summer, you may have to subtract an hour to adjust for Daylight Savings Time. Check your sundial at different times during the day to see how well it's keeping time.

9. In your left hand, hold the cardboard dial folded in half as shown. In your right hand, hold a triangle piece with the 90° angle on top and the angle of latitude (L) on the right as shown. Fit the triangle into the folded cardboard dial. Tape it securely with masking tape.

N

12. As a final touch, decorate your sundial. You can write a message on it. In eighteenth-century gardens, sundials carried warnings such as "It's later than you think."

How does it work?

Sundials work because the Earth makes one complete turn every day, going through a full 360° turn in 24 hours. Therefore the Earth turns 360/24 or 15° in one hour. Every hour, the shadow cast by the gnomon moves 15° around the dial.

BABYLONIAN COUNTING

It's Perfect!

Why is a circle made up of 360° instead of a nice round number like 100? It all started with the Babylonians, who lived about 4000 years ago near present-day Baghdad in Iraq. We normally count things in units of 10, but the Babylonians counted in 60s. So they divided the circle into 360 equal parts called degrees (60 times 6). Their method of counting by 60s affects your life in other ways, too — the dials on your clocks and watches are marked into 60 minutes because of Babylonian counting.

The Babylonians found the number 360 handy because so many whole numbers divide evenly into it. Not 7 or 11, but there are 23 other numbers that do. To measure the 360 degrees of a circle, you need a special instrument called a protractor.

Concentric circle dazzlers

Here are some cosmic-looking circle designs to try. Use wild colours, and the lines of contrasting colour will shimmer and dance before your eyes.

You'll need:
a pencil
a compass
lined paper or graph paper
a ruler
2 contrasting colours of coloured markers — for example, red and green or orange and blue

1. Draw a series of 10 concentric circles (circles with the same centre) an equal distance apart. It's easiest to start with a small circle and then use the lines on the paper as a guide to show you how much to increase the radius for the other circles.

2. Draw a vertical diameter through the largest circle.

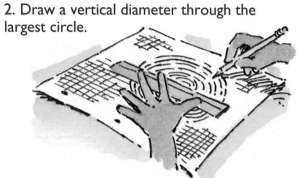

3. Use markers to colour the areas within the lines, alternating colours in a checkerboard pattern as shown.

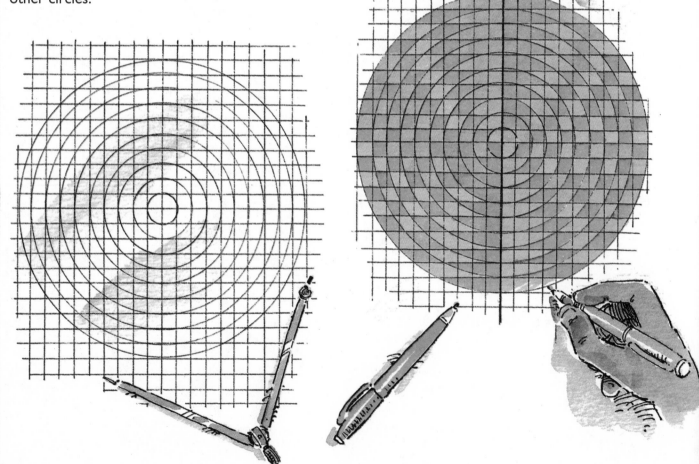

As a variation, try this design of intersecting circles. It's like the pattern formed by two stones thrown into a still pond.

1. Turn a piece of lined paper sideways. Draw a straight line horizontally across the middle of the page.

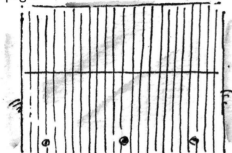

2. On this line, about a third of the way from the left edge of the paper, mark a dot. With this dot as the centre, draw 14 concentric circles (circles with the same centre) an equal distance apart. Use the lines on the paper to show you how much to increase the radius of each bigger circle.

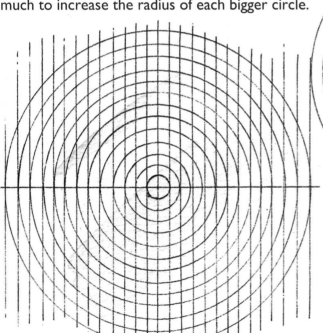

3. At the point where the ninth circle intersects the horizontal line, mark a second dot. Use this dot as the centre of 14 more concentric circles identical to the first.

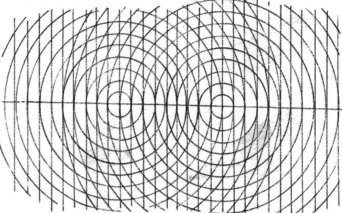

4. Use markers to colour in alternate areas as shown. The checkerboard pattern you create will reveal an ellipse.

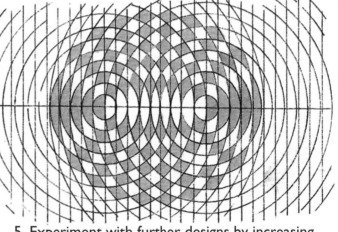

5. Experiment with further designs by increasing the distance between the centres of the circles.

4 Spheres

Spin a coin around fast on its edge. Presto, a sphere or ball-shape — a circle in three dimensions. So what's so special about a sphere? Every place on its outside surface is exactly the same distance away from its centre. This means you can cut a slice through a sphere anywhere and always get a circle. Try for yourself by cutting slices through an orange or grapefruit.

The sphere is also special because it's so compact — it has the least possible surface area or outside skin to contain its volume. That's why hibernating bears curl up into balls to sleep through the winter — this way they lose the least body heat and stay warmest. It's also why designers make spherical teapots. Heat is lost from a teapot through its outside surface. A spherical teapot loses its heat slowly because it has the least possible outside surface area.

For most of us, the best thing about a sphere is the way it rolls. With every place on its outside surface the same distance from the centre, spheres such as marbles and bowling balls roll smoothly in all directions.

The big blue ball

If your eye is 2 m (6 feet) above the water, you can see 5 km (3 miles) out to sea. At 17 m (54 feet) above the water, you can see 15 km (9 miles). And at 46 m (150 feet), you can see 24 km (15 miles).

What's the biggest sphere you can touch? You're standing on it! The Earth. Some people used to think that the Earth was flat, but sailors have known for centuries that the Earth is a sphere. When another ship approaches over the horizon, only the top of its mast can be seen at first, then the whole mast, and finally the entire ship. To see distant ships sooner, lookout sailors used to climb up the rigging into the crow's nest at the top of the mast. Because the Earth is a huge ball, you can't see forever, even on a clear day. But the higher the point you look from, the further out you will be able to see.

Mapping Earth

Take a good look at a world map. It's rectangular with 90° corners, right? So how do you draw a spherical world onto a flat, rectangular map? Find out by turning your breakfast grapefruit into a flat map. Imagine that the grapefruit is the Earth, and the middle of the grapefruit is the equator. The top and bottom of the grapefruit can be the poles.

You'll need:
a kitchen knife
a grapefruit
a breadboard

1. Put the grapefruit on the breadboard and cut it in half.

2. Cut a series of thin slices until you have cut up the whole grapefruit.

3. Cut through the white part between the fruit and the rind, so that you end up with rings of grapefruit rind.

4. Cut through each of the rings to form strips. Lay out all the grapefruit strips as shown.

Your grapefruit map gives you a picture of the surface of the grapefruit. But it doesn't look like a real map because it isn't a rectangle. To make your map rectangular, you'd have to stretch out the shorter strips near the grapefruit's "poles."

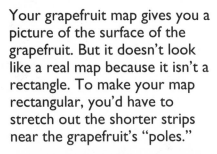

The Dutch mathematician Gerard Mercator was the first map maker to solve the problem of showing a spherical world on a flat map. The map he made in 1569 projected the spherical world onto a cylinder. He had to stretch out the top and bottom of his map. That's why places at the Earth's poles, such as Baffin Island and Greenland, look bigger on Mercator maps than they really are in relation to other places.

GREAT CIRCLES

If you cut an orange into slices, which slice would you want? Probably the slice from the middle, because it's the biggest. Circles that go through the centre of a sphere are called great circles (all the rest are small circles). A great circle is any circle that divides a sphere into equal halves. The best-known great circle on the planet Earth 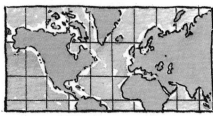 *is the equator. Great circles can be drawn on the globe in any direction so long as they go through the Earth's centre.*
Navigators on airplanes need to know about great circles because flying a great circle route saves fuel. That's because a route on a great circle is always the shortest way between any two points on the Earth's surface.

Bubbles

What's the easiest sphere you can make? The soap bubble. Soap bubbles turn out perfectly round every time, without any special skill or talent on your part. That's because the soap film is like an elastic skin around the air inside. The soap film tries to contract as much as it can, while at the same time the pressure of the air inside is pushing out. So a soap bubble becomes a sphere — the shape with the least possible outside surface area to contain the volume of air inside. Make some perfect spheres every time with this recipe for super-bubbles.

You'll need:

1 L (4 cups) of lukewarm water
150 mL (2/3 cup) of dishwashing detergent
15 mL (1 tbsp.) glycerine, available in drugstores (optional, but it makes the bubbles stronger)
a large flat container such as a plastic dishpan
1 m (3 feet) of string made of a material that stays wet (cotton and jute work well, but not nylon)
2 plastic drinking straws

1. Mix the water, detergent and glycerine gently together in your container. Don't make a lot of suds.

2. Make a bubble frame by threading the string through both straws. Tie the ends together. You now have a giant bubble frame with two straws for handles.

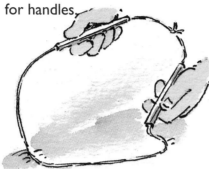

3. Take your bubble mixture and bubble frame outside to blow the bubbles.

4. Wet your hands in the bubble mixture. (Dry hands break bubbles.)

5. Dip the entire bubble frame in the bubble mixture. Lift it out carefully so that you don't break the film.

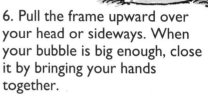

6. Pull the frame upward over your head or sideways. When your bubble is big enough, close it by bringing your hands together.

P. S. If you want just enough bubble mixture to make small bubbles, you can mix together 250 mL (1 cup) of lukewarm water and 15 mL (1 tbsp.) detergent. For an easy bubble-blower, make two short cuts in the end of a straw and splay out the cut ends.

BUBBLE ARCHITECTURE

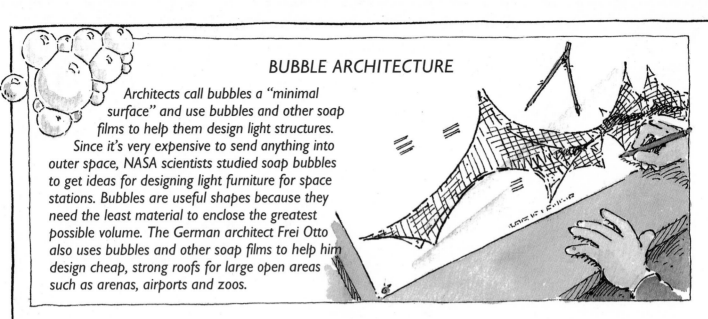

Architects call bubbles a "minimal surface" and use bubbles and other soap films to help them design light structures. Since it's very expensive to send anything into outer space, NASA scientists studied soap bubbles to get ideas for designing light furniture for space stations. Bubbles are useful shapes because they need the least material to enclose the greatest possible volume. The German architect Frei Otto also uses bubbles and other soap films to help him design cheap, strong roofs for large open areas such as arenas, airports and zoos.

Bubble packing

One bubble is a perfect sphere. But what happens if you have two or three or a whole bunch of bubbles all touching each other? To find out, make some suds.

You'll need:
some bubble mixture
a glass
some water-soluble paint, such as poster paint
a straw
some white paper
waxed paper

1. Put some bubble mixture in the bottom of the glass. Add a small amount of paint and stir.

2. Use a straw to blow into the bubble mixture until bubbles form over the top of the glass.

3. Blow the bubbles off the glass so that they fall on the white paper. Don't let the bubbles fall anywhere else — they'll leave a paint mark. (If the bubble pattern on the paper is too faint, add more paint, stir and try again.)

4. Experiment with different sizes of bubble clusters. When the bubble marks dry, you will be able to see what happens when different-sized bubbles come together.

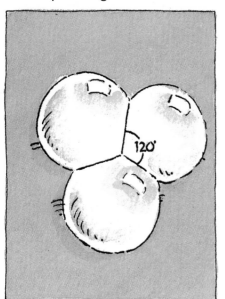

5. Next put some bubble mixture on the waxed paper to dampen it. (Bubbles won't break on a wet surface.)

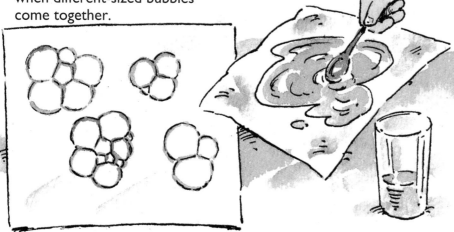

6. Put your straw into the bubble mixture. Take it out and blow a single bubble. Place the bubble on the dampened waxed paper.

7. Blow another single bubble and place it carefully beside the first bubble on the waxed paper.

8. Add a third bubble. Notice how the three bubbles come together.

How does it work?

If you had a jar of marbles, you would see air spaces where the marbles do not fit together. Unlike marbles in a jar, bubbles are elastic and can squash together to fill all the empty spaces.

Two bubbles come together to share a flat wall. But three bubble walls always meet at 120° angles because this arrangement uses the least amount of bubble film to enclose the air inside.

Soap bubbles always come together in threes. You can find this same three-way pattern in honeycomb walls and in mud cracks when mud puddles dry out.

HONEYCOMBS

Take a look at this honeycomb. It sure looks as if bees must be geometry experts to make these honeycomb patterns. Actually, honeycombs form into hexagons exactly the same way that bubble clusters do. The cells of the honeycomb start off as circles. But under the pressure of being packed closely together, the circles flatten out and become hexagonal to fill all the available space.

CLOSE PACKING

Scientists study Ping-Pong balls and oranges to discover how shapes fit together to fill space. For example, equal-sized spheres pack together so that each sphere touches or "kisses" 12 others. In this closely packed arrangement, oranges in a crate can fill up three-quarters of the space inside — the rest is air.

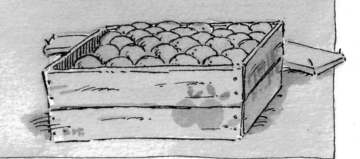

Let's play ball!

Which sphere is the most fun? The ball — which comes in all kinds of sizes, colours and materials. Games of marbles, baseball, basketball, tennis, bowling, not to mention golf, Ping-Pong and soccer all use balls. What's so special about the ball? For starters, its centre of gravity (balance point) is at its exact centre. Check this for yourself by balancing a basketball on the tip of your finger. The trick is to keep your fingertip exactly under the centre of the ball.

Rolling games such as marbles, croquet and bowling would be a disaster without the ball. Ever try rolling something rectangular, like a milk carton? Balls roll better than milk cartons because each point on the outside of the ball is the same distance from the centre. So balls roll smoothly while milk cartons bump along. Another good thing about the ball is that it touches the ground at only one small point. This cuts down on the drag, or friction, so the ball rolls easily. Give a ball and a milk carton each a good push, and the milk carton soon grinds to a stop while the ball keeps on going.

Losing your marbles

See how far and straight you can shoot in this marble game. People all over the world have played marble games — Aztecs, Romans, Chinese, Africans, Europeans and North Americans. Here's one you can play at home.

You'll need:
a coloured marker
6 empty containers of different shapes and sizes, such as milk cartons, cereal boxes, yoghurt and ice-cream containers
equal numbers of marbles for each player (5 to 10 marbles per player works well)
string

1. Use a coloured marker to number each container from 1 to 6 in order of size. Label the biggest container 1, label the next biggest 2, and so on to the smallest container, which is 6.

2. Arrange the containers in a line, alternating bigger containers with smaller ones. These containers will be your targets. Face the open ends towards the shooting line, where the shooters will stand.

3. Agree on a shooting line some distance from the targets such as 3 m (10 feet) — further if your players are expert. Mark the starting line with a piece of string.

4. Players take turns shooting one marble at any of the targets. If the marble goes into the container and stays there, the player's score is the number on the container. (It doesn't count if the marble bounces out.)

5. When the players use up all their marbles, they add up their total scores. The one with the highest score wins.

Super Domes

What do you get when you cut a sphere in half? Two half spheres (hemispheres) or domes. The dome is one of the strongest shapes there is. Test its strength by squeezing an egg. Put an uncooked egg lengthwise between your palms and push with all your might. You won't be able to break it — honest. The two dome shapes that make up the egg are stronger than you are.

The oldest houses were dome-shaped huts of mud and straw, and we still use dome shapes to make high-tech tents as well as roofs for big sports arenas. Here are some spectacular domes. Can you think of any dome-shaped buildings where you live?

An Inuit family on the move can build an overnight dome, or igloo, of snow blocks in about an hour. First they outline a circle about 3 m (10 feet) in diameter. Then they build the igloo from blocks of snow cut carefully to just the right size and shape. The completed dome is strong and can be heated with just one small oil lamp to a comfortable temperature — just below freezing.

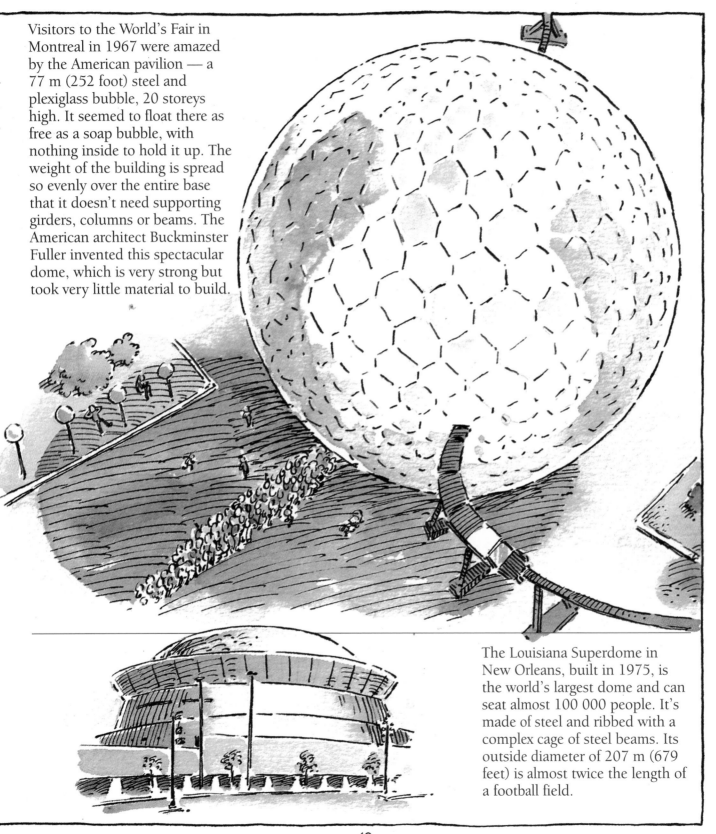

Visitors to the World's Fair in Montreal in 1967 were amazed by the American pavilion — a 77 m (252 foot) steel and plexiglass bubble, 20 storeys high. It seemed to float there as free as a soap bubble, with nothing inside to hold it up. The weight of the building is spread so evenly over the entire base that it doesn't need supporting girders, columns or beams. The American architect Buckminster Fuller invented this spectacular dome, which is very strong but took very little material to build.

The Louisiana Superdome in New Orleans, built in 1975, is the world's largest dome and can seat almost 100 000 people. It's made of steel and ribbed with a complex cage of steel beams. Its outside diameter of 207 m (679 feet) is almost twice the length of a football field.

Make your own domes

When you make buildings out of blocks, you get straight walls and right angles. Try using circles as your building material, and you'll create some fabulous curved constructions.

You'll need:
a compass
a pencil
some Bristol board or
   cardboard
a ruler
a paper punch that makes a
   single hole
scissors
a heavy piece of cardboard or
   some layers of newspaper to
   protect your table
a box of 5 cm (2 inch) elastics

1. Set your compass feet about 12 cm (5 inches) apart and draw a circle on the Bristol board.

2. Use the radius of the circle to mark six division points on the circumference (see p. 26). Draw a line to join every other division point. You have outlined an equilateral triangle — its sides are the same length.

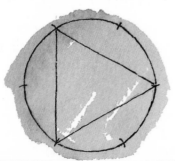

3. Use a ruler and the point of the compass to score, or cut, along the outline of the triangle on the circle. Don't push so hard that you cut right though the cardboard.

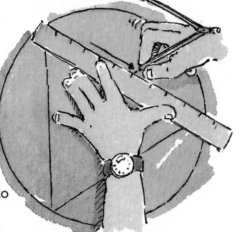

4. Cut out the circle.

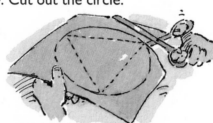

5. Cut holes at the corners of the triangle with a single-hole paper punch.

6. Fold along the sides of the triangle. Now you have a building unit.

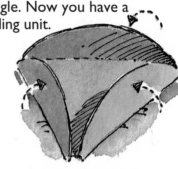

7. Make at least 10 more of these building units the same way.

8. You are ready to start construction. Place two units side by side as shown. Join them by fitting an elastic around the flaps so that they are held by the punched holes.

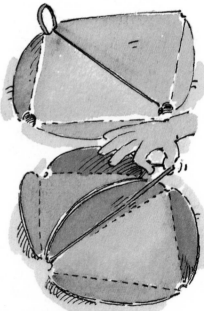

9. Experiment with different shapes. What do you get when you join four building units together around a central point? How about five? Six?

10. With 20 units, you can make a dome shape called an icosahedron. With more, you can make elaborate curved structures. When you want to dismantle your creation, remove the elastics and store your building units for next time in a big plastic ice-cream container.

5 Discs

Make a round ball of Plasticine or other modelling clay, put it on a table and flatten it out. You've made a disc. This disc has a lot more surface area than your original ball — it takes up more space on the table. Discs are circles with a little thickness to make them three-dimensional. Turned on its rim, a disc will roll like a wheel. Balance a disc such as a paper plate on the tip of your finger and you will discover that its balancing point is the centre. Having a disc shape is often an advantage. Round flat cookies, for example, cook in the oven faster than ball-shaped ones, because they have more surface area exposed to the heat.

Chip discs

These discs are so delicious they don't last long. Experiment with disc-shaped and ball-shaped cookies.

Equipment:
a large mixing bowl
a measuring cup
a wooden spoon
a mug
measuring spoons
a fork
2 baking sheets
a pancake lifter
oven mitts

Ingredients:
125 mL (1/2 cup) softened
   butter or margarine
125 mL (1/2 cup) white sugar
125 mL (1/2 cup) brown sugar
1 egg
5 mL (1 teaspoon) vanilla
2 mL (1/2 teaspoon) salt
2 mL (1/2 teaspoon) baking soda
250 mL (1 cup) flour
250 mL (1 cup) rolled oats
125 mL (1/2 cup) chopped
   walnuts or pecans or
   sunflower seeds (optional)
250 mL (1 cup) chocolate chips

1. Ask an adult to turn on the oven to 190° C (375° F).

2. Put the butter (or margarine) in the large mixing bowl.

3. Add the white sugar and the brown sugar to the butter. Use the wooden spoon to mix the sugar into the butter until the mixture is creamy-coloured.

4. Break the egg into the mug. Add the vanilla, salt and baking soda. Beat together with a fork.

5. Pour the egg mixture on top of the butter mixture and beat until well mixed together.

6. Stir in the flour, using the wooden spoon. Add the oats and nuts and stir again.

7. Add the chocolate chips and stir in with the wooden spoon.

8. Roll pieces of the dough into golf-ball-sized balls. Make about 12 balls for each baking sheet.

9. Use the pancake lifter to flatten some balls into discs; leave some as balls.

10. Bake your cookies for 8-10 minutes.

11. Use the oven mitts to take the baking sheets from the oven. Use the pancake lifter to place the cookies on a clean flat surface to cool.

12. Did the discs or balls cook better? Decide which cookies you like best and bake the rest the same way.

Pinwheel dics

You'll need:
a piece of thin cardboard
a pencil
scissors
a stapler
a straight pin
a plastic straw

1. On the cardboard, draw a square shape as shown and cut it out. A square with a 15 cm (6 inch) side works well.

2. Cut along the dotted lines as shown.

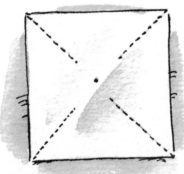

In Holland, rotating discs on windmills use wind power to pump water from low-lying land. Discs catch the wind because, like sails, they have a lot of surface area. In fact, the earliest windmills used canvas sails instead of slatted wooden arms for the rotating disc. Later, wooden arms were mounted on a pivot so that they could always face into the wind. Find out about the power of wind by making this pinwheel disc.

3. Bend the four corners into the centre to form a pinwheel and staple it.

4. Push a pin through the centre of the pinwheel and then through one end of a straw.

5. Bend the pin over at the back to keep it from falling out.

Blow on your pinwheel. Which direction does it spin — clockwise or counter-clockwise? Which way does it work better — when you blow from the front or from the side?

MEMORY DISC

How do you store 350 000 pages of text? Build a new library? No, put it all on a CD-ROM disc and you'll save in paper the equivalent of 17 black spruce trees. A CD-ROM is a 120 mm (5 inch) silicon disc. It looks like a regular compact disc that plays music, but it can hold a whole multi-volume encyclopedia. The letters CD-ROM stand for compact disc read-only-memory. This means that you can play the disc but you can't record new information on it.

SAILING SEEDS

Wind turns windmills and also carries seeds long distances through the air. Since plants are anchored by their roots to one spot, they need to ship off their seeds to open places where new plants can find light and growing space. So some seeds are equipped with special disc-shaped gliding equipment or rotating wings.

• The maple key's single wing rotates in a circle around the seed so that it spirals downward, slowing its fall. A good breeze can carry maple keys 200 m (665 feet) away from the parent tree before they reach the ground.

• Slippery elm seeds are shaped like discs to glide through the air.

Super flyer

Make your own super flyer to test out how well discs fly.

You'll need:

scissors
2 paper plates
masking tape

1. Cut the flat centre out of one paper plate to produce a plate rim like this.

2. Place the plate and the plate rim together so that the rims touch.

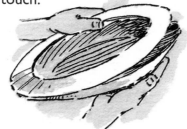

3. Tape the plate to the plate rim using eight short pieces of masking tape as shown.

Test this super flyer outside. To launch it, hold it as shown, with your thumb on top and your fingers curled under the rim. Throw it backhand, with a snap of your wrist. With the wind behind it, your super flyer should really zoom.

Experiment with some other disc-shaped flyers that you can find in your own kitchen — plastic plates, metal lids or tops of plastic containers. Give them a test spin to see which ones go furthest. Flying distance will depend on factors such as the size, shape and weight of the disc, your throwing power and, of course, the wind.

Tops

You can turn a disc into a spinning top by putting a stick through its centre. Experiment with spinning objects by making this top. If you draw a spiral pattern on your top, it will seem to expand or contract when it spins.

You'll need:
a compass
a pencil
a piece of cardboard
scissors
a piece of white paper
2 markers of contrasting colours
glue
a round cocktail toothpick (not the flattened kind)

1. Use the compass to draw a circle with a radius of 5 cm (2 inches) on the cardboard. Cut out the circle.

2. Draw the same sized circle on white paper.

3. Colour your paper circle. Starting at the circumference, use one of your coloured markers to draw a spiral as shown (see page 70 to find out more about spirals). Leave approximately the width of a pencil between each turn, until you reach the centre. Go over the coloured line with your marker until you have made the coloured area just as wide as the white space in between.

4. Fill in the white space with the contrasting colour.

5. Cut out the circle and paste it onto the cardboard circle to make a coloured disc.

6. Use the point of the compass to poke a hole in the centre of the disc. Push the toothpick through the cardboard about 1 cm (1/2 inch). The toothpick works as the axis or pivot for your top.

7. Launch your top. Set it off by spinning it between your thumb and index finger. The more force you apply during the launch, the longer the top will spin. Try clockwise and counter-clockwise spins.

8. Invent your own tops by putting together various handy materials. For a larger top, you can use plastic lids from yoghurt containers. Use a pencil instead of a toothpick for the axis.

What makes a difference to how well a top spins? Experiment by raising and lowering the height of the disc on the pencil that is the axis. Make a heavier top by using several layers of material for the disc. Make a top with a bigger diameter.

How does it work?

How long a top will spin depends on its weight, the distribution of the weight and the launch speed. Tops balance better when their weight is kept low down, just as skiers crouch low to keep their balance. Heavier tops spin for longer than light tops, but they are harder to launch. Wide tops spin for longer than narrow tops. And all tops spin faster and longer when launched at higher speeds.

A GIANT TOP

The world itself moves like a giant top. It spins on an imaginary line, called the polar axis, which goes through the north and south poles. The rotation of the Earth is gradually slowing down. Now it takes 24 hours and 4 minutes for the Earth to make a complete turn on its axis, but 400 million years ago it took only 22 hours. So days then were two hours shorter.

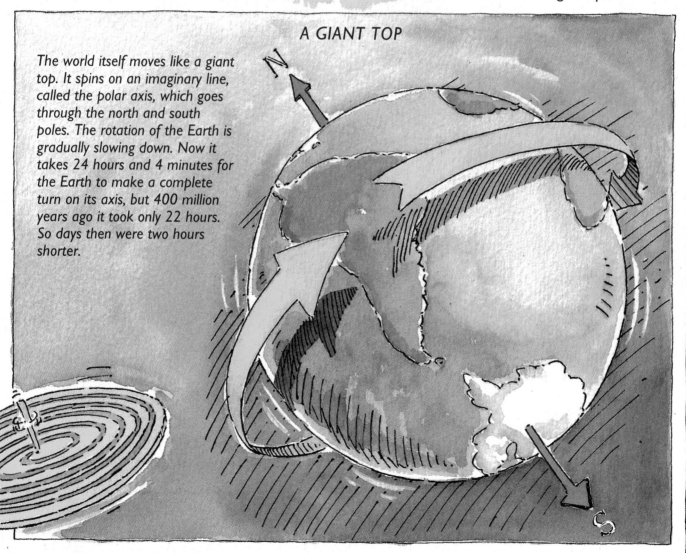

Wheels

What do you think was the most important invention ever? Fire? A metal axe? Ice cream? How about the wheel? Without the wheel, you wouldn't have cups, plates and bowls made on a potter's wheel. There would be no cars, bicycles or roller skates. Like all circles, wheels have radial

symmetry, and that's what makes them so useful.

Who invented the wheel? Cave dwellers drew wheel-shaped pictures on cave walls to represent the sun. But people didn't use wheels for anything practical until about 4000 BC, when the potter's wheel and the

Rollers Egyptian pyramid builders and the makers of Stonehenge used circular rollers to move huge stone blocks from the quarries to the building sites.

Solid wheels The first wheels were made of three rectangular boards fastened together into a square and then rounded off at the corners. Early people didn't make wheels from slices of logs because they didn't have metal saws. But cross-sections of logs wouldn't work very well as wheels anyway because they would split apart along the grain.

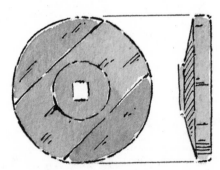

Spoked wheels Between 2000 BC and 1500 BC, spoked wheels were invented and used for chariots. Made of a hub and rim connected by spokes, these wheels were lighter than solid wheels and provided a faster, smoother ride.

wheeled cart were invented. When the Spaniards came to Mexico after Columbus's discovery of the New World, they were amazed to find that the Aztecs made pottery toys with wheels but they didn't use wheels for transportation. Why not? Because wheeled carts aren't much use unless there are some large, strong, tame animals around to pull them. There were no horses or oxen in North and South America before Europeans brought them across the ocean. So Aztecs used llamas instead and loaded packs on their backs.

The inventor of the wheel figured out that it took less energy to roll something along the ground than to drag it. Wheels work by reducing friction — the result of one thing rubbing over another. Some friction is useful. Without it, your feet would slip out from under you as you walk. (People slip on banana peels because there's not enough friction between the shoe and the banana peel.) But too much friction wastes energy and slows movement. The wheel is the perfect friction beater.

Wheels and axles The earliest wheels were firmly attached to their axle — when the wheels turned, the axle turned too. About 100 BC, a big improvement was the rotating wheel that spins freely on an axis that doesn't turn. This design cuts down on friction.

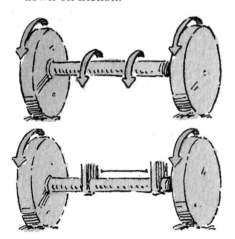

Inflatable rubber tires John Boyd Dunlop patented the first "pneumatic" rubber tire in 1888 as a way to make bicycles ride more smoothly. Early bicycles were sometimes called "boneshakers" because their metal wheels gave such a bumpy ride, even when covered with solid rubber tires. Dunlop came up with the revolutionary idea of fitting the wheel with an inflatable rubber inner tube protected by a rubber tread.

BACTERIAL WHEELS

No animals have ever evolved wheels to roll on instead of legs. That's because a wheel has to turn freely, like a bicycle wheel, and so it has to be separate from the body. There would be a big problem of connecting the nerves and blood vessels in the wheels to the nerves and blood vessels in the rest of the body. Bacteria have evolved the closest thing to wheel travel. E . coli. bacteria move by rotary motion. A threadlike flagella, like a little tail, rotates at 6000 turns a minute and pushes the bacteria along.

6 Cylinders

Can you think of some cylinders in your home? How about cans, paper-towel rolls, broomsticks, pencils, paint rollers and rolling pins? Outside there are tree trunks and telephone poles. And did you know that the long bones in your legs are cylindrical columns? Even polar bear hairs are very thin cylinders, hollow like a drinking straw. Air trapped inside the hair is such a good insulator that it keeps a polar bear's skin warm even in the Arctic.

Cylinders are circles that have been stretched out into a column. The top and bottom of a cylinder are parallel circles. You can make a cylinder by rolling a rectangular piece of paper into a tube, taping the tube together and covering the ends with circles.

A cylindrical soup tin can't hold as much soup as a spherical container would with the same outside surface area. But it's a hit in grocery stores anyway, because its flat bottom keeps it from rolling off the shelf.

Be an architect

If you were an architect and wanted to stay in business, you'd have to design strong buildings that wouldn't fall down. So you'd need to know which shapes support weight best and stand up well to pressure. Try this experiment to find out what shapes make the best supports for buildings.

You'll need:
13 x 8 cm (5 x 3 inch) index
   cards
masking tape
a stack of paperback books

1. Form a cylinder by bringing the two short ends of a card together, overlapping slightly. Tape the ends together with masking tape.

2. Now make a square column. Take a second card and make a very narrow fold parallel to one of the short ends. This makes a tab for taping. Now fold the rest of the card in half so that the other short end touches the first fold line. Fold each half in

half. Fold your card into a square column and tape down the tab.

3. Now for the triangular column. Take a third card and again make a very narrow fold to form a tab. Fold the rest of the card into three equal sections. Fold into a triangular column and tape down the tab.

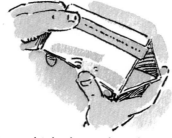

4. Test which shape does best under pressure by gently squeezing the sides together.

5. Now test the strength of each of these columns. Carefully place paperback books, one at a time, on top of one of the columns. Keep adding books until the card collapses; record how many books were supported. (If the column falls over because the books weren't balanced properly, that doesn't count. Try again.) Next test the strength of the other two

columns in the same way. Each time, record how many books the column supported. Which shape was the winner?

How does it work?
The strength and stiffness (resistance to bending) of material depend on its shape. The secret to a hollow column's strength is how far its material is spread out from its central axis — the centre of the column. In fact, the hollow cylinder is the strongest shape there is. It's a lot stronger than a solid rod made of an equal amount of material. A hollow bamboo stem can grow as high as 37 m (120 feet) without collapsing under its own weight. The leg bones of the elephant and the brontosaurus are hollow cylinders, too — they'd have to be to support that much weight!

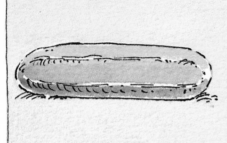

Can you slice a cylinder into these shapes?

You'll need:
an English cucumber (or a banana)
a paring knife
a slicing board
(See page 80)

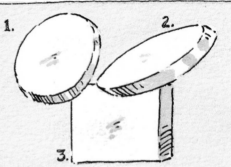

1.
2.
3.

Castles

Ever wonder why castles have those grand-looking towers? They actually have a purpose. Builders in Europe started to build more castles with cylindrical towers in the fourteenth century — just after European armies started using cannons. With this new weapon, an invading army could fire cannon balls at a castle wall from a safe distance, pounding it steadily to pieces. So builders redesigned fortresses with thicker walls and cylindrical towers.

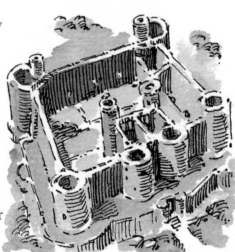

Round cannon balls go right through a flat wall. But they tend to roll off a curved cylindrical one.

Cylindrical towers at the corners of a castle have another advantage, too — they're harder to dig under. A favourite trick of attacking armies was to dig a big hole under the castle walls right at the corner. If walls meet to form a corner, then one hole can cause two entire walls to fall down. This doesn't happen so easily when walls are built in a circle.

WHAT'S MY AGE?

You've likely seen a tree stump or the cross-section of a tree, with its many concentric circles. These circles are the tree's growth rings. Each year, a tree grows a new circle outside last year's ring. The ring grows fastest in the spring, slows down in summer and finally stops growing in the fall and winter. Since the rapid spring growth is lighter in colour than the slower summer growth, each year's growth shows up as a separate ring. (Except at the equator, of course, where there is no difference in the amount of sunlight during the year and therefore no growth rings.)

If you want to know how old the tree is, you have to count the rings at the base of the tree, not *at the top. That's because a tree trunk grows like an upside-down cone, with a new cone added on top of the old one every year. So there are fewer rings at the top of the tree than at the bottom.*

Tricks with cylinders I: Chicken wire

It's easy to roll a flat piece of paper into a cylindrical tube. You can use the tube to spy through or shout through. Or you can use it to make this intricate chicken-wire pattern — it just takes a few pinches.

You'll need:
a piece of paper (any size from a small square to notepaper size will work)

1. Roll the paper into a tube about 1 1/2 cm (1/2 inch) in diameter.

2. With the thumb and finger of your left hand, pinch one end of the tube to flatten it. Keep pinching with your left hand.

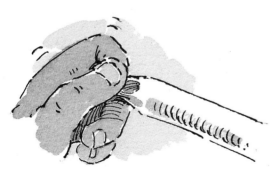

3. With the thumb and finger of your right hand, pinch the tube at right angles to the first pinch. Your second pinch should be as close as possible to the first pinch.

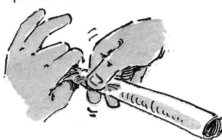

4. Push the two pinches together to make the creases as sharp as you can.

5. Make a third pinch at right angles to the second one. Push the second and third pinches together to sharpen the creases.

6. Continue in this way, making pinches at right angles to the previous one until you have put pinches in the whole tube.

7. Carefully unroll the tube.

8. If you want to make the pattern easier to see, outline the crease marks with black marker.

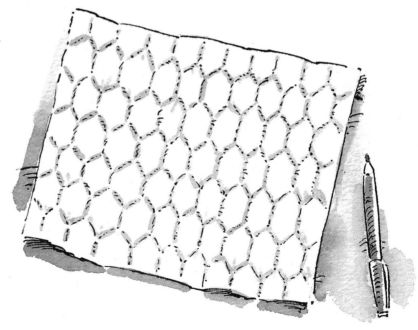

You can send a secret message to a friend using a code invented by the ancient Spartans in Greece. For years they were at war with the citizens of Athens. When they wanted to send messages that the Athenians couldn't read, they used a cylinder cipher. They would wrap a leather belt tightly around a stick (called a scytale) and then write on the belt along the length of the stick. When the belt was unwound, all that appeared was a meaningless jumble of letters. But someone with another stick exactly the same size could rewind the belt and read the message. You can make your own version of the Spartan scytale.

You'll need:
paper and scissors
transparent tape
2 new pencils the same size

1. Cut a strip of paper about 1 cm (1/3 inch) wide and 30 cm (12 inches) long.

2. Use tape to attach one end of the strip to a pencil. Wind the strip of paper tightly around the pencil as shown, so that the edges of the paper touch.

3. Secure the other end with tape so that the strip doesn't unwind while you are writing your message.

4. Write your message along the length of the pencil. When you get to the end of the line, turn the pencil and start a second line.

5. Unwind the paper strip carefully. Can you read what it says?

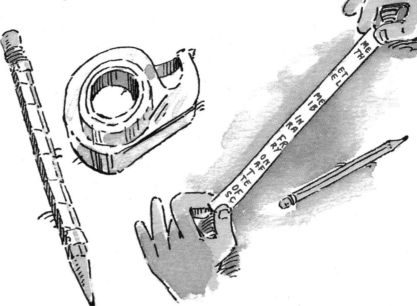

6. Rewind the strip to read the message.

You can send messages this way to anyone who knows how to crack the code.

7 Cones

The best thing about cones is that you can put jamoka grape ice cream in them. But there are some more good things about cones:

• The biggest sand pile that you could possibly build on a given area of land would be in the shape of a cone. Volcanoes, which are like giant sand piles, are cone shaped.

• Cones roll, but not in a straight line as spheres and cylinders do. Place a cone on its side, and it will turn in a circle around its pointy end, or vertex. That's why birds that lay eggs on stone ledges often have cone-shaped eggs — these eggs roll in circles around their small end but they don't roll off the ledge.

Cones get top marks for stability. Check this out. Take a cone-shaped drinking cup and try to knock it over.

Cone hats

If you need a special hat for a costume party, start by making a circle, then turn it into a cone.

You'll need:
a pencil
string
large sheets of coloured paper (thick paper or Bristol board works well, but you can also use double pieces of newspaper)
scissors
sticky tape

1. Use the pencil and string method (page 7) to draw a circle with a radius of at least 25 cm (10 inches). Mark the centre of your circle with a dot.

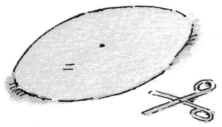

2. Cut out the circle.

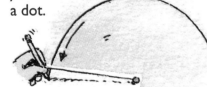

3. Make a cut from the outside of the circle to the centre.

4. Give the circle a quarter turn and make a second cut from the outside to the centre. Remove the quarter-pie-shaped piece or sector.

5. Tape the edges of the larger piece together. Now you have a sun hat like the hats worn by rice planters in China.

6. If you want a pointier hat, cut out another circle the same size with a radius of 25 cm (10 inches). Cut the circle in half. Tape the edges together and you have a clown's hat. To make a really pointy witch's hat, start with a much bigger circle. The radius of the circle is always the length of the side of the hat. Experiment with different sizes.

7. If you made your hat from newspaper, paint it with poster paint to add some pizazz.

What's happening?
You have turned a two-dimensional circle into a three-dimensional cone. Stand your hat on a table. The point, or vertex, of the cone is directly above the centre of the circle that forms the base or bottom of the cone.

Slicing a cone

If you cut a flat slice off the bottom of a cone, you get a circle. But cones can be sliced in other ways to make some unexpected curves or shapes. An ancient Greek mathematician, Apollonius, discovered these shapes, called conic sections.

Circle Make a cut parallel to the base.

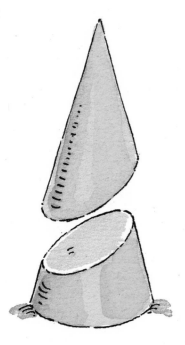

Ellipse Make a cut at an angle to the base.
Kepler discovered that the planets move around the sun in an ellipse. Halley's comet makes an elliptical orbit around the sun, coming back every 76 years close enough for us on Earth to see it.

Volume of a cone

How many cones does it take to fill a cylinder of the same base and height? (See page 80 to find out.)

Hyperbola Make a cut perpendicular to the base.
Some comets follow paths that are hyperbolas. Unlike Halley's Comet, these comets don't come back but keep on going further and further into space. The shadow on the wall made by a cylindrical lampshade is a hyperbola.

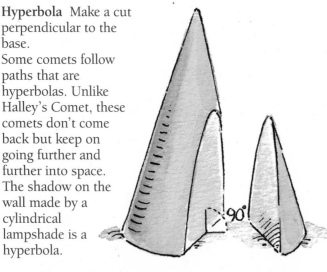

Parabola Make a cut parallel to the side.
Water coming out of a hose and balls flying through the air travel in a parabola.
Cables supporting a suspension bridge are parabolas.

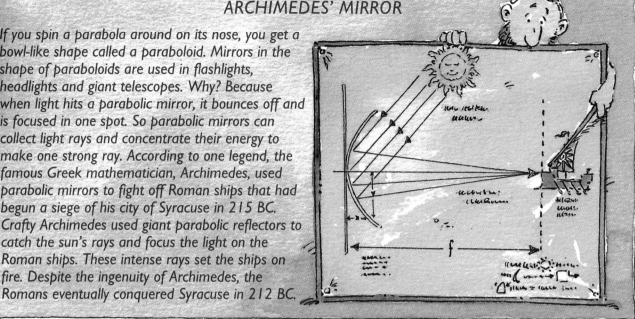

ARCHIMEDES' MIRROR

If you spin a parabola around on its nose, you get a bowl-like shape called a paraboloid. Mirrors in the shape of paraboloids are used in flashlights, headlights and giant telescopes. Why? Because when light hits a parabolic mirror, it bounces off and is focused in one spot. So parabolic mirrors can collect light rays and concentrate their energy to make one strong ray. According to one legend, the famous Greek mathematician, Archimedes, used parabolic mirrors to fight off Roman ships that had begun a siege of his city of Syracuse in 215 BC. Crafty Archimedes used giant parabolic reflectors to catch the sun's rays and focus the light on the Roman ships. These intense rays set the ships on fire. Despite the ingenuity of Archimedes, the Romans eventually conquered Syracuse in 212 BC.

Hyperbola folding

You can make a hyperbola by folding paper.

You'll need:
a compass
a pencil
a piece of paper

1. Use your compass to draw a circle with a radius of about 10 cm (4 inches) on a piece of paper.

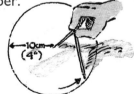

2. Choose a point outside the circle and mark it with a dot.

3. Fold the paper so that the circumference of the circle touches the dot. Crease the paper.

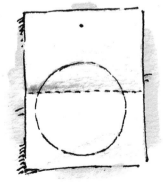

4. Work your way around the circumference of the circle, making more folds in your paper. Make sure that the circumference touches the dot each time.

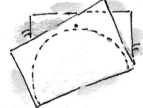

5. Eventually the crease lines form a hyperbola. As you can see, parabolas come in two parts—two curves which are mirror images of each other.

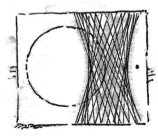

8 Spirals

What do a coiled snake and a spider's web have in common? They're both spirals. A spiral is an open curve that keeps on growing (unlike the closed circle where the end meets the beginning). When something grows steadily out from a centre, it becomes a spiral — like a spider's web or the horns of a big-horned sheep. Since a spiral doesn't end, it's a good shape for an animal that grows bigger at one end, like a snail or a chambered nautilus. A spiral can also be the shape of a spin — like the water going down a drain or the funnel of a tornado.

Another kind of spiral is the equiangular spiral. Its coils constantly get wider from one turn to the next.

A good example of the equiangular spiral is the snail. As the creature inside grows, it makes its house bigger by adding on new material to the growing edge. The coils get wider as they move out from the centre, but the shell itself doesn't change its overall shape. What makes the snail shell coil? The secret to its spiral turning is that the outer edge of its growing surface grows faster than its inner edge. The chambered nautilus and the ram's horn also grow this way into an amazing spiral shape.

But if you think all spirals are the same, look a bit closer. There are really two different kinds of spirals. The Archimedean spiral (named after the same Greek inventor who was so clever about parabolas) gets bigger at a steady rate. The distance between each turn stays the same, as it does in a coiled rope. You'll also find the Archimedean spiral in a spider's web. A spider starts her web by spinning out a framework, which she fills in with spokes. Then from the centre point, she goes around and around, keeping the same distance between each turn. And then, presto! an Archimedean spiral just waiting to catch a fly.

Party spiral

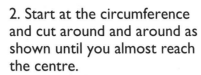

Turn this spiral into a party decoration.

You'll need:
a compass
a ruler
a piece of coloured paper at
   least 20 cm (8 inches) square
scissors
a piece of thread
coloured markers

1. Draw a circle with a radius of about 10 cm (4 inches) and cut it out.

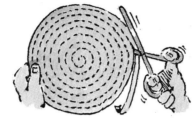

2. Start at the circumference and cut around and around as shown until you almost reach the centre.

3. Use the sharp end of the compass to poke a hole through the centre.

4. Loop a piece of thread through the hole and hang up your spiral. If you think it needs more pizazz, you can decorate it with markers first. Hang it up over a heat source, and your party spiral will rotate.

Fibonacci numbers

1 1 2 3 5 8 13 21 34 55 89 144 233 377 610 . . .
These numbers are special — they follow a pattern. Can you figure out how these numbers are related? (See page 80 to find out if you're right.) This string of numbers, called the Fibonacci number series, gets its name from the greatest European mathematician in the Middle Ages — Leonardo of Pisa, nicknamed Fibonacci, which means son of Bonacci.

But the Fibonacci numbers are not just a neat math trick; they also describe how leaves, flowers and branches grow. Leaves often grow around a central stem in a spiral that follows Fibonacci numbers: five leaves in three turns around the stem, eight leaves in five turns. If you count the petals on flowers, you will discover Fibonacci numbers. The most common number of petals is five. Marigolds and daisies have 13, 21 or 34 petals. (Since daisies usually have 34 petals, which is an even number, you're likely to get bad news when you pull out petals, saying "She loves me, she loves me not.") Try your own petal count of different flowers.

When plants grow by adding on new parts similar to their old parts, they form spirals. Pine cones are spirals and so are the heads of daisies and sunflowers. If you cut through the bottom of a bunch of celery, you find the stalks arranged in a spiral. These spirals are pretty amazing — the numbers of stalks in these spiral arrangements are almost always Fibonacci numbers.

Oh sunflower!

Check out the Fibonacci series for yourself and grow some birdseed at the same time.

You'll need:
a place in your garden that gets lots of sun all day
a trowel or small shovel
a package of sunflower seeds
some Popsicle sticks or other markers
a container of water

1. In the spring when the danger of frost is past, dig some holes about 10 cm (4 inches) deep and 1 m (3 feet) apart.

2. Put three or four seeds at the bottom of each hole. Cover over the seeds with earth and press the soil down firmly.

3. Mark the holes where you planted the seeds with a Popsicle stick so that you'll

remember where they are. Water the seeds and keep watering as needed. You should see the first sprouts in about two weeks.

4. When the plants are 10 cm (4 inches) tall, remove the smallest, weakest plants to leave just one plant in each hole. This way each plant will have room to grow. Sunflower plants look small at the beginning, but by August they may be 2 to 3 m (6 to 9 feet) tall!

What's happening?

Watch how the sunflower itself develops. That big disc looks like a single flower, but it's actually hundreds of disc flowers packed together in a head. If you look carefully, you will see that each disc flower is a tube made of five petals fused together. These produce the seeds.

When the disc flowers wither in August, you can see that the seeds are arranged in two interlocking spirals, one whirling counter-clockwise and the other whirling clockwise. Average-size sunflowers have 34 counter-clockwise spirals and 54 clockwise spirals. But some giant sunflowers have 89 spirals and 144 spirals. A Vermont gardener reported a mammoth sunflower with 144 spirals and 233 spirals. Fibonacci numbers again!

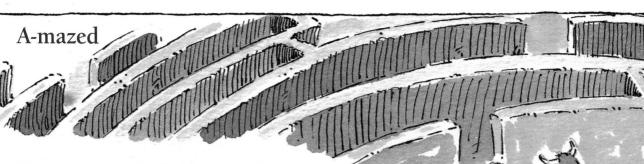

A-mazed

Mazes are tricky paths that you can get lost in. Spiral mazes have an enclosed inner space that is hard to find. You can't go directly to the centre, but have to spiral round and round through confusing turns to get there. Once you're inside the maze, it's even harder to find your way back out again. For thousands of years, people have had fun with mazes. They have carved spiral maze patterns onto rock, made mazes from small stones and planted garden mazes.

The most famous maze of all was built by the legendary King Minos of Crete, an island in the Mediterranean Sea. King Minos hired Daedalus to build a "labyrinth," or maze, to be the home for a monster called the Minotaur. This Minotaur was half man and half bull, very ferocious and very hungry. Young men and women who were put into the labyrinth were his favourite dinner. Finally Theseus from Athens decided to kill this horrible monster, but he couldn't have done it alone. King Minos's daughter, Ariadne, who loved him, supplied Theseus with a special sword and a ball

of thread. "Tie one end of the thread at the entrance," she said, "and unroll the ball as you go along." When Theseus got to the centre of the maze, he killed the Minotaur with Ariadne's sword. Then he escaped from the spiral maze by following the thread back to the entrance.

In memory of the labyrinth of King Minos, people have made labyrinths or mazes that are big enough to walk through. In the Middle Ages, tile mazes were built inside European cathedrals like the one in Chartres Cathedral in France. Later, rich people had their gardeners plant hedge mazes on their estates. At Hampton Court Palace near London, England, there is a famous hedge maze with paths almost a kilometre (half a mile) long where thousands of people get lost every year. The next time you go to a sandy beach, you can make a maze for yourself and your friends to get lost in. With a big stick, trace out this spiral design or experiment with designs of your own. Make it tricky to find the correct path into the centre and out again.

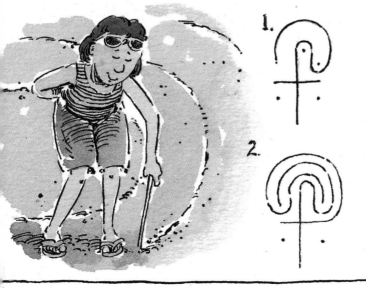

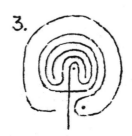

1.

2.

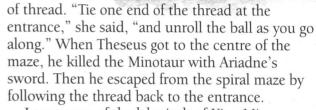

3.

4.

9 Be a circle!

Next time you make an angel in the snow or sand, look closely at the impression you have made — it looks like a circle. The famous painter and inventor, Leonardo da Vinci, made a famous drawing of the human body fitting inside a circle inside a square. He published it in 1509 in a book on mathematics.

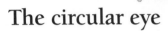

The circular eye

The first circle shape we see when we are babies is the eye. Psychologists have discovered that newborn babies are attracted to any round shape with two black round spots on it. A smiling face is best, but babies will also look intently at a mask with two black beads attached to it as long as the beads are side by side.

The eye shape, used as a decoration, has the power to protect. Primitive people made beads ornamented with round spots — friendly eyes — to ward off evil spirits or the "evil eye." Ancient Egyptians made "eye beads" decorated with spots with rings around them to imitate the iris of the eye. Even butterflies, birds and fish have taken advantage of the protective power of the eye. When the peacock butterfly opens its wings, four big eyes that seem to belong to a very large animal glare out at enemies and scare them away. The peacock can't fly fast or sing well, but for centuries the hundred eyes in its tail-feather pattern made it a royal bird of the East, strutting around in princely gardens. The butterfly fish that lives on coral reefs has a big fake eye at its body's tail. Sometimes to confuse its enemies, it will swim backward. But when it really wants to escape, it swims frontward — opposite from the way its enemy expects.

In a spin

Spin around fast five or six times and then stop suddenly. How do you feel? As if the room is whirling around? You get this dizzy sensation because the semi-circular canals in your middle ear have been tricked. These canals, which are filled with fluid, normally help you keep your balance. Any movement of your head sets the liquid moving in the semi-circular canals of your inner ear and stimulates small hairs at the ends of the canals. These hairs are connected with nerve fibres that send a message to tell your brain where your body has moved. This system of balance normally works well. But if you spin around, the fluid in the semi-circular canals eventually will be moving at the same rate as you are. You feel okay while you're still spinning, but, when you stop, the liquid in your ears is still turning, stimulating the hairs. The signals from these hairs tell your brain you are still moving but your eyes are telling your brain that you are standing still. The result? Vertigo, which means dizziness.

So why don't ballet dancers and figure skaters get dizzy? Olympic skaters such as Brian Orser have been clocked at up to nine complete turns a second.

The three semi-circular canals are set at different angles so that they can detect movement in any direction.

The prima ballerina in Swan Lake has to make 32 turns in a row. Ballet dancers and skaters both have learned special tricks to ward off dizziness. Dancers use a technique called spotting. At the beginning of a spin, the dancer fixes her eyes on a spot in front of her. As her body turns, her head stays facing frontward, with her eyes on the spot, for as long as she can. Then she quickly turns her head around until she can focus on the spot again. For most of the spin, her head is still. The liquid in the semi-circular canals moves only for the brief period of the spin when she is whipping her head around. This time is not enough for the liquid to reach a state of constant spinning. So even making two or three turns a second, a ballet dancer doesn't get dizzy and fall.

Skaters spin so fast that they can't keep their eyes fixed on one spot. Instead, they are taught to keep their head in line with their body as they spin. Although a skater's eyes may be open, they don't focus on anything. When the spin is over, the skater fixes his skates firmly in the ice and tosses his head in the opposite direction from the spin. This head toss prevents dizziness by stopping the motion of the liquid in the semi-circular canals of the ear.

Circle race

In a race down a slope, which do you think would win — the disc, the sphere or the ring? Try this circle race to find out.

You'll need:
a wide smooth board, such as a
   piece of plywood
a metal washer (with a hole
   inside)
a nickel
a marble

1. Set up your board on a slope.

2. Line up two contestants on a starting line at the top of the slope. Let go of both at the same time and observe which one reaches the bottom first. (If a contestant falls over, begin the race again.)

3. To find the final winner, line up the third contestant against the winner of the first race.

4. Check to see if this win was just a fluke by running the race over again.

How does it work?
Did your marble win the most races? It's got to do with the weight of the marble and where the weight is distributed. The further its weight is spread out from the centre, the slower an object rolls. That's why the washer won't roll as fast as the nickel and the nickel won't roll as fast as the marble. The marble is fastest because it has all of its weight as close as possible to its centre of rotation.

Distribution of weight is also the key to why a skater spins faster when he pulls in his arms. A skater starts his spin with his arms stretched out. Then he pulls his arms in tight to his body, so that more of his weight is close to his centre of rotation. This makes him speed up. If you're not an Olympic skater, you can experience the same effect in a swing. Sit in the swing and turn yourself around about 10 or 15 times. When the rope holding up the swing unwinds, you will start to spin. Control your speed by extending your legs out from the centre of rotation and then by bringing them in.

ROUND TABLES

King Arthur's knights sat at a round table to show that they were all equal. At a rectangular table, the person who sits at the head of the table is usually the big boss. But when the table is a circle, there is no head. There is no first and no last in the circle. Everyone is equal.

Glossary

Angle the V-shape formed by two straight lines that intersect at a common end point

Arc a part of the circumference of a circle

Area the amount of surface of a closed, flat shape such as a circle or rectangle

Bisect to divide in half

Chord a straight line joining two points on the circumference of a circle

Circumference the distance around a circle

Concentric circles circles in the same plane having the same centre

Diameter a chord that goes through the centre of a circle

Ellipse a closed curve looking like a flattened circle produced when you slice through a cone at an angle to the base

Geometry the study of the size and shape of things

Hemisphere half of a sphere

Intersect to share at least one point in common. For example, two straight lines can intersect at one common point

Parallel lines two lines in the same plane that do not intersect

Perpendicular lines two lines that intersect at right angles or 90°

Pi (π) the number you get when you divide the circumference of a circle by its diameter

Plane a flat surface

Radius the distance from the centre to any point on the circumference of a circle. The plural is radii

Rectangle a four-sided polygon with four right angles

Right angle a 90° angle such as the corner of a square

Rotation a motion that turns an object around a fixed point or centre

Sector of a circle a pie shape outlined by two radii and an arc of a circle

Solid a three dimensional figure such as a sphere, cylinder or cube

Volume the amount of space inside a solid

Circle formulas

π is 3.14.

The circumference of a circle is $2\pi r$ ($2 \times \pi \times$ radius).

The area of a circle is πr^2 ($\pi \times$ radius $\times$ radius).

The surface area of a sphere is $4\pi r^2$ (4 times the area of a circle with the same radius).

The volume of a cylinder is $\pi r^2 h$ ($\pi \times$ radius $\times$ radius $\times$ height).

The volume of a cone is $1/3\ \pi r^2 h$ ($1/3 \times \pi \times$ radius $\times$ radius $\times$ height).

The volume of a sphere is $4/3\ \pi r^3$ ($4/3 \times \pi \times$ radius $\times$ radius $\times$ radius).

Index

Answers

Slicing cylinders, page 62:

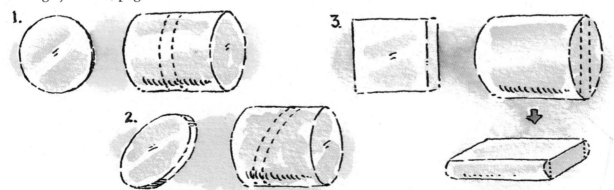

Volume of a cone, page 68:
It would take three cones to fill the cylinder. The volume of a cylinder is exactly three times the volume of a cone with the same base and height.

Fibonacci numbers, page 71:
Each number in the series is the sum of the two previous numbers. Thus, 2+3=5 and 5+3=8 and 8+5=13 and 13+8=21 and so on.